THE SOCIAL IDEALS OF ALFRED TENNYSON AS RELATED TO HIS TIME

BY
WILLIAM CLARK GORDON

HASKELL HOUSE
Publishers of Scholarly Books
NEW YORK
1966

PREFACE

The following pages were written originally as a thesis for the degree of doctor of philosophy at the University of Chicago. It was suggested by certain interested friends that the subject-matter herein contained might be of value to the students of sociology and of literature included in a larger public than is usually reached by the conventional thesis. The publication of this little volume is the answer to these kindly suggestions.

The author ventures to hope that readers into whose hands this book may chance to fall may derive from its perusal some of the pleasure and profit that was his in acquiring and shaping its material. The footnotes should be omitted by everyone who does not wish to make it a text-book. These, however, will be found a necessity by the careful student and will suggest the rich stores left in the ink-pot.

The union of sociology and literature here exemplified and defended is, we believe, more than justified. It is to be commended. The work here attempted is capable of almost indefinite extension, and, if entrusted to competent hands, may prove of great service to each department. This is a rich field for the student, and it is already white unto harvest. The task involved is not for the novice, but for the one trained in the peculiar methods and familiar with the facts and principles of both literature and sociology. It is to be earnestly hoped that master-workmen may in due season thrust their sharpened sickles into these waiting fields and gather therefrom rich and abundant harvests.

W. C. G.

TABLE OF CONTENTS

CHAPTER I

LITERATURE AS A MEANS OF SOCIAL EXPRESSION ·

It is by no means universally admitted that literature has any value for the student of social science. The litterateur is, as a rule, dominated by the artistic ideal. He insists that his art has a value in and of itself, entirely independent of any utilitarian purpose it may serve. He frequently resents any effort on the part of the social philosopher to seek in his domain for facts out of which to construct a theory of society. He finds little justification for the attempt to set in relief the essential features of the associated life of the people whom he, as a literary artist, has wrought into his picture of the time.

To affirm that literature is a field in which the student of society has a perfect right to seek for facts of real significance for his own science, is to arouse the opposition of certain zealous defenders of literary art. For the sociologist to go farther, and actually use for his own purposes the material which has been wrought into drama and novel and poem by the skilful hand and inspired imagination of the maker of literature, is to commit what is considered a flagrant offense by some guardians of high artistic standards. To go even farther, and seek for the ideals by which the literary artist himself is governed, the object which he endeavors to accomplish, the motives determining his choice of scenes and characters, times and places, " to live inside the artist and see him breathe," and then persistently to ask for the social significance of this inner life of dramatist, novelist, and poet — that is by some considered an outrage.

Yet the literary artist is not a more constant or wilful violator of the command, " Thou shalt love thy neighbor as thyself," than are other men. His zeal in defending his realm against the invasion of those whom he considers foreigners and barbarians is perhaps excessive, but he is contending for a principle which is in every way worthy of his most strenuous endeavors. The continued existence and exaltation of his art are dependent upon the successful maintenance of that principle. He demands that literature shall be something more than a tool in the hands of a clumsy reformer. It is to him something sacred, and is not to be " soiled by all ignoble use." He knows well enough that, if literature were to become merely a bludgeon in the hands of garrulous cranks and fanatical propagandists, it would instantly cease to be literature. Literary history gives abundant proof of the direful results of such misappropriation of the form of literary expression by those who have some pet theory to advance, or some supposed reform to advocate. The modern homily in verse or prose even the most charitable cannot call art. Samuel Richardson in 1740 published *Pamela* with an avowedly didactic purpose, but no one today would hesitate to say that his work would have been more successful, if his purpose had been less didactic and more artistic. The didactic novel or poem belongs to an earlier and lower stage in the development of literature than the work of artistic purpose. To return to that earlier and lower type would be in every sense a calamity. To literature this would mean the substitution of some very poor preaching for some very good art, and it is no secret that the supply of poor preaching in the world's market today is much greater than the demand. Further production of a commodity of which there is already an over-supply would be a misfortune, and ought to be discouraged by all who have at heart the real interests of society. In this general calamity sociology would share.

Literature and sociology need to understand each other. They are not competitors, but partners. The closeness of their relationship has not been generally recognized, and is not recognized today, but it is none the less real and vital on that account.   Sociology would have quite as good a right to guard its borders, and open fire upon the wandering trespassers and tramps of literature who seek to forage in the ill-defined fields of the science of society, as has literature to oppose the efforts of the sociologists to gather from fiction and poetry material to be made of social service.   The standards of literature are scarcely in greater danger of being lowered by the prosaic loquacity of the sociologist than are the standards of sociological science by the graceless inaccuracies and watery imaginings of much that purports to be literature.   If the sociologist is met by the taunt that he cannot define his own science, he replies by asking the student of literature: What is literature?   The period of silence that follows may well be employed by both questioner and questioned in earnest reflection upon the infinities and the limitations of his own department of special study.   Each department has over its head an infinite heaven to which it is related, and under its feet a fertile soil in which to dig.   Both may well give heed to the words of Carlyle, who was himself both a writer of literature and a student of society: " Let every man mind his own business, and do that for which he was made."

Sociology, then, may be pardoned if it does not assume an apologetic attitude in seeking in literature valuable material to be used in its own department as it deems best.   A man does not apologize for taking what belongs to him. Taunts and ridicule are not called for by the conditions existing in either department.   If sociology cannot define itself, neither can literature define itself; for who can point to a definition of literature which is universally accepted?   There is no occasion for criticism in this.   Tennyson declares that "nothing can be defined that is worth defining," and it may be because these departments of knowledge are both so well worth defining that thus far definition has seemed impossible.   Literature is old.   Sociology, as a distinct science, is comparatively new.   What literature has not been able to accomplish for itself in centuries, sociology has failed to achieve for itself in the comparatively few years of its existence as a distinct branch of knowledge.   If literature has suffered in its artistic quality by being made simply the vehicle of some social propaganda, sociology also has suffered by the misrepresentations of makers of literature who have done much to strengthen the foolish impression that sociology means feeding tramps and going slumming.   The literary pot may well hesitate to dwell too long and eloquently upon the blackness of the sociological kettle.

The attitude of hostility or of condescension on the part of either toward the other is entirely without justification. It wholly misrepresents the true relation of these two great departments of human knowledge and of social service. They are really friends, and are mutually helpful. As a matter of fact, they are now rendering invaluable assistance to each other, though neither recognizes its indebtedness to the other. The removal of this ignorance would mean the removal of much of jealousy and foolish criticism. Emerson knew that " light is the best policeman." It is also the best judge, arbitrator, peacemaker. It is certainly to be hoped that in the near future some one who combines the literary insight of Frederic Harrison with the social wisdom and breadth of Thomas Hill Green may reveal to us the close and vital connection between these two great branches of the tree of knowledge.

In this study the point of view is primarily that of the student of society, and only secondarily that of the student of literature We ask: How does literature minister to social progress? What estimate is to be placed upon it as a means of social expression? These questions are, of course, entirely distinct from such queries as this: What service has sociology rendered to literature? — a most interesting inquiry, which only a volume could answer satisfactorily. Frederic Harrison, speaking of the literary production of the Victorian Era, says: " Our literature to-day has many characteristics; but its central note is the dominant influence of sociology — enthusiasm for social truths as an instrument of social reform." [1]   And again: " For good or for evil, our literature is now absorbed in the urgent social problem, and is become but an instrument in the vast field of sociology — the science of society." [2]   This is certainly of interest as indicating the opinion of one writer of authority concerning literature's debt to sociology. Miss Vida D. Scudder, in *Social Ideals in English Letters,* has given distinct and intelligent recognition to the same indebtedness in a much wider field of English literature.   Both of these writers are skilful literary critics, but the latter, at least, is not known to have specialized to any extent in the department of scientific sociology. It is probably not too much to say that both Mr. Harrison and Miss Scudder have written from the standpoint of literature rather than that of sociology.

One may well question the literal accuracy of Mr. Harrison's statement that our literature " is become but an instrument in the vast field of

[1] *Studies in Victorian Literature,* p. 13.
[2] P. 26.

sociology." That is certainly putting too strongly the truth which every student of literature must recognize. That the interests of man as man, and that the interests of society, are finding literary expression as never before is undoubtedly true, though it would be impossible to deny that social interests of some kind have been represented in the literature of every period. The difference is one of degree rather than of kind. The attitude toward what we call social questions in the literature of any period is in general a reflection of the time in which the book was written. Some writers of fiction and of verse represent the advance guard, and some the stragglers, in the army of progress; but in general they hold the mirror up to their own time. The materialization in literature of the mirrored image is of great significance to the student of society, for there he can find concretely portrayed the men and the manners, the conditions and the conflicts, the thoughts, feelings, and ideals, which write social history. Even before the days of Pope and Swift and Richardson and Fielding, social history was being thus written, and since their time the remarkable development of the novel and other forms of literary expression has given greatly increased opportunities for the faithful representation of social facts and forces.

It would not be safe to rely *wholly* upon poets

and novelists for our knowledge of the social conditions of any period.   The view of an epoch acquired entirely from this source would be as one-sided and inadequate as a view obtained from the study of history alone.   History and literature may be, and should be, correctives of each other.   In fact, if certain modern critics are right, very few histories have ever been written. Most books called by this name have been merely records of the accessions and dethronements of rulers, and statements of the dates of great battles, of the numbers killed and wounded on each side, and of the final result in victory and defeat for one side and the other.   Because of the skilful manipulation of the figures by historians of different parties or nationalities, we are sometimes left sadly in the dark as to what the real facts were.   Figures that " cannot lie " are often used by lying men, and the result is, to say the least, bewildering.   But, as Mr. John Graham Brooks, among others, has pointed out, the great and all-important periods of peace and prosperity and progress have too often found no historian at all.   Battles, which are mere ripples upon the surface, have been described over and over again with scrupulous care, while the great surging tides of thought and desire that cause the surface movements of the waters, and carry the ripples upon their bosom, have too often been utterly ignored.   When history shall have been restudied and rewritten, both literature and sociology will have, in history so written, a storehouse of material which will be invaluable for their respective uses.   Whether this new history shall be written by men who call themselves historians, or by men who call themselves sociologists, is of comparatively little importance.   We want the results; let who will do the work.

Let us frankly recognize, then, that literature is not the only source of knowledge of society, though it is an important one.   Let us emphatically assert that the opinions formed as a result of the study of this material need to be corrected by facts gained from philosophy and history, and many other departments of knowledge.   It yet remains true that literature is one of the important documents to be studied by the person who wishes to know the social conditions or developments of any period.   In some cases it furnishes perhaps the best means of knowing thoroughly the life and thought of an epoch.   If we ask the reason of this, we find the answer, first, in the character of literature itself; secondly, in the work which literature actually accomplishes; and, thirdly, in the methods by which literature achieves its results.   Of these the second is by far the most important.   The analysis and discussion of this work which literature accomplishes in the portrayal of social life will occupy the larger part of this study.

I

First as to the character of literature. Really effective art does not obviously strive after effect. The actor who plays to the pit may win howlings of applause, but he is not contributing to the exaltation of his art or the permanency of his own reputation. The painter who works for the medal and colors his canvas to please the whim of some influential member of the committee may gain the coveted bronze, but he sacrifices his artist instincts and ideals. What does it profit an artist to gain all the trinkets that were ever stamped into hideousness, if he loses the seer's vision and the artist's power to suggest and portray? The one who poses or who lowers, for any cause whatsoever, what to him is the very highest standard of effort, by that act proves his lack of appreciation of what is highest and most enduring in his art. The real alone is permanent. As the perfect comes the partial is done away, and to leave any work less perfect than it is possible to make it is to render it to that degree transient and insufficient.

The first demand that sociology makes upon literature is that it shall be true to the highest

artistic standards.   We have said that if literature were to become, as Frederic Harrison declares it has become, " but an instrument in the
vast field of sociology," the result would be as
disastrous to sociology as to literature.   Literature is valuable to the student of society because
of its unconsciousness, its spontaneity.   It speaks
to us while off its guard.   Here as everywhere
the truth is the ultimate standard by which a
work of art must be judged.   The writer does
not make a conscious effort to portray truth in
the abstract, nor does he hold himself rigidly to
the recital of particular facts or occurrences; but
there are certain great principles to which he
yields obedience, consciously or unconsciously, if
his work is really successful.   It must be " true
to life," as the hackneyed phrase puts it — true
to the laws of nature, thought, imagination, emotion.   If, in his endeavor to advocate a theory,
he disregards these laws, his work loses wholly
or in part its artistic quality.   The laws may
not be clearly defined.   There may be a difference
of opinion as to the validity of any one of them,
but there remains a residuum that is real, though
ill defined.   To these laws the true artist is obe-
dient by instinct as often as by conscious effort.
The portrayal of life in harmony with these great
principles is the task which is given him by the

ideals of his art, and by his own tastes and desires.

The serviceableness of literature to sociology is, we repeat, almost wholly dependent upon the faithfulness of literature to the artistic ideal in the portrayal of life. Mere description of physical conditions and statement of social facts have their value, but it is the psychical elements for which the sociologist looks most eagerly and which he studies with greatest care. He wishes to know of what people have been thinking; what ideals they have cherished for the home and for the government; how they have regarded woman; what attitude they have taken toward those of different rank and social station; what desires have exercised a controlling influence in the lives of men and women; how the emotional life has expressed itself — all these and a hundred other things of kindred nature are of very great importance to the student of human associations. He insists that literature shall not pose. When men are not talking for effect, they say what they mean, and such talk indicates the psychical life of the speakers. That is to say, sincerity and simplicity are as essential in art as in religion and everywhere else in life. When a man says within himself, " Go to now, I will be pious to-day," he usually makes of himself either a hypocrite or a fool. He seeks to cover himself with a mantle which has no vital connection with his real self, or he wheedles himself into the belief that he can actually be one man one day in the week and an entirely different man the other six days.   Corresponding hypocrisy and folly in the writer of literature make his work of no value to the sociologist.   Sunday piety in literature is valueless in any state of the market.   Sociology asks, and has a right to ask, that novel and poem be true to their own highest ideals, obey the laws of their art, and portray the inner and the outer life as these are in reality or in potentiality.

The demand that literature be true to the very highest artistic ideal, that it never lend itself to the mere propaganda of any doctrine or theory social or otherwise, does not, on the other hand, imply that novelists and poets should keep themselves aloof from the conditions which are the subject of social inquiry, and the forces which are producing great social movements.   Perhaps writers could not do this if they tried.   It certainly would not be desirable if they could.   Most books are written primarily for their own age rather than for all ages.   They ought to reflect their own time as well as all times.   This is not in any sense a limitation upon their possibilities, but a means of greater efficiency and power. Ruskin has taught us, with no doubtful emphasis, that truth and sincerity are primary requisites of all noble art, and surely the present of the artist is not without its truth to be expressed. To ignore or reject it is to lose an element of great power and value. The writer of literature is under obligation, not to sociology, but to his art, to enter into the intellectual and emotional struggle of his time and to give to these the most perfect artistic expression of which he is capable.

II

The value of literature to the student of society is largely explained by the work which literature actually accomplishes. If, now, we ask, What does literature do which gives it this value as a means of social expression? we get a three-fold answer. First, it studies the *past* with most scrupulous care, and gives, or seeks to give, a truthful portrayal of the life of that past time, often showing facts and tendencies which persist in the present. To do this effectively, the writer must know something more than the battles fought and the acts of parliament. He must study the conditions existing at the time of the great events which many so-called historians merely state and date. He must know the hills and valleys, the meadows and rivers, the farms and the roads, the barns and the houses, the methods of life, the men and the women in their inner and their outer lives, their loves and their

hates, their religion and their crimes, their customs and their conventions, their mental strength
and weakness, their emotions, passions, superstitions, morality, and everything else that con-
cerns the physical or the psychical life of the
people among whom the writer, in imagination,
lives and moves and has his being.   There is
no one who is obliged to study a past epoch more
carefully, more in detail, or more comprehensively
than the writer of literature.   He has to go to
many sources for his material, and, when gained,
the various elements must be fused into unity by
the power of imagination and made to breathe
again the breath of life.   When we remember
the many important epochs of the past which
have been thus recovered to us by novelists and
poets, we begin to appreciate the greatness of
our indebtedness to these benefactors of the race.
Then, when we think of that subtle, indefinable
something which we call the " spirit of the time,"
the presence of which in prose or verse does so
much to make, and the absence of which does
so much to unmake, literature, we are still further impressed with the difficulty and the delicacy
of the task which the literary artist has to perform.   Unless this work is well done, it is of as
little value to the sociologist as to the general
reader.

One of the results of the study of the past is

the discovery of certain principles of progress which are of permanent value. Sometimes these results are negative, but chemistry and biology and other sciences have taught us that some negative results may be of as great practical value as some which are termed positive. Ignorance of these negative results is the explanation of the repetition of many profitless experiments in charity, legislation, and industry under conditions similar to those in which they were formerly tried without success. The waste of time, effort, and money from this ignorance is enormous and inexcusable. While it is not one of the chief functions of literature to give information concerning the fruitless attempts of the past to meet social needs which, so far as we know, are permanent, as a matter of fact the novels of the latter half of the eighteenth century do record facts concerning prison reform, education, church life, the relations of classes, etc., a knowledge of which would be most helpful to the student of society today. These facts are recorded, not as items in a dry chronicle, but as expressions of the life of the time, and are given in their natural social and psychical relations. They are seen to be effects of which the causes are the conditions, sympathies, desires, ideas, of the people. They are not unrelated happenings.

Some positive principles are, however, almost

certain to emerge from various efforts directed
toward the solution of a vexed problem.   Negative results — failures, so called — to the critical
student are indices pointing to the principles
which must be embodied in action, if the desired
results are to be obtained.   Methods are not given
in detail, and no patent devices are warranted to
produce infallible and miraculous results.   Usually failures and partial successes are the necessary first steps to more complete and perfect triumph obtained after the lessons of failure, partial or complete, have been learned.   Even then
the triumph is not so perfect as our theories, and
a priori arguments would indicate that it should
be; for while experiments have been tried, conditions have been changing, and they compel new
adjustments and adaptations.   The new wine of
principle cannot be put into old bottles of method
without disastrous results to both.

The study of the past shows also certain *tendencies* which were not pronounced enough to
be expressed in great events or in legislation,
but which nevertheless were real and important.
This drift is clearly revealed, whether the literature be the embodiment of the present through a
spontaneous and unconscious expression of its
ideals, or the rehabilitation of the past through
the historic imagination.   It requires no very
close or accurate knowledge of our time to under-

stand that there is today a socialistic tendency, meaning by that a tendency to the acceptance of the theory that the products of labor should be more equally distributed through the public collective ownership of land and capital, and the public collective management of land and capital.[3] Even Spencer believed this and trembled. Yet we are confident that this is not, after all, a sudden growth. The present conditions are perfectly natural in the sense that they have come about in strictest accordance with law. But to go back a few decades and discover the acorn out of which this mighty oak has grown, to find the influences, silent and unseen, which watered and nourished it — this is quite a different matter. This is what literature does for us, not perhaps consciously, but none the less really. In the conversation of peasant and priest and lord; in the attitude assumed by representatives of different classes toward each other; in the aspirations expressed by the poets of the people; in the vague longings and unsatisfied desires; in the questionings of what men call " providence; " in the ideas of right, the appeals to justice — in all these are the prophecies of changed conditions, and the future dominance of different theories of life and property. These sources of change and progress are studied, understood, and expressed

[3] *Standard Dictionary,* " Socialism."

by the writer of literature as, perhaps, by no one else, though he may be as ignorant as others of their real significance for the future. But, standing actually or in imagination in the midst of the age of which he writes, and being keenly sensitive to the subtle but effective influences of thought and emotion, he *feels* as well as knows and writes, so that his words have life as well as information.

The value of this method of presentation of truth, as contrasted with that employed by the historical or scientific chronicler of fact, is appreciated by Mr. Frederic Harrison, who protests against " the flat, ungainly, nerveless style of mere scientific research." He continues:

What lumps of raw fact are flung at our heads! What interminable gritty collops of learning have we to munch! . . . . It would seem as if the charge which some of our historians are most anxious to avoid is the charge of being "readable," and of keeping to themselves any fact they know. . . . . They [the scientists] are accustomed to lecture to students in the laboratory in their shirt sleeves, with their hands in their pockets; and they believe that immortality may be achieved if they can pile up enough facts and manufacture an adequate number of monographs.[4]

There is reason for insisting that literature possesses real scientific value for the student of

* *Victorian Age,* p. 20.

society simply because it has interest and vitality, and because its ideas are well expressed. It makes revelations of the silent influences and tendencies that increase in power until they find expression in laws, events, and institutions. These revelations are not less true because they are made with purity of diction and with genuine human interest.

It follows, as an inevitable corollary of the above, that literature performs a social service of very great value in calling attention to crying wrongs that ought to be righted and abuses that ought to be corrected. In any particular case it is almost impossible to tell who first comes to a realization of the injustice involved in any social condition or custom, or who first gives expression to the sense of wrong which is often more felt than reasoned. The mere matter of priority is of little practical importance. It is important, however, to recognize that literature is one of the most effective means of calling attention to social evils and bringing about a better state of things. It performs this beneficent service in various ways, but especially by compelling recognition of unpleasant and hidden facts, stimulating investigation, creating public opinion, and arousing public conscience. It is often affirmed today that this work is done by the pulpit and the newspaper. There can be no reasonable doubt that there is much to be said for this claim; but this is not saying that literature is not an efficient agent operating in the same field. The statement gives us no information as to the indebtedness of the pulpit and newspaper to literature for information concerning conditions and for stimulus to effort. Because this indebtedness is often indirect rather than direct, it does not cease to be real.

Literature is practically serviceable in the first stages of a reform rather than in a later, and therefore often fails to receive its due meed of praise. After attention has been called to a social evil, and people have been made to feel the wrong, the work of formulating and enforcing laws is done by others. Those who see only the visible results in legislation and social action forget the steps that had to be taken before the first act could be introduced into the legislative body with any hope of success. The fact that the successful writer of fiction and of verse is more sensitive to the changing conditions, thoughts, and emotions of men than others, makes him a pioneer in the work of social transformations. He feels sooner than others the desires, ambitions, and aspirations which struggle for expression, and which are the sure prelude of social changes corresponding to this psychical condition. Certain classes in society have often waited long for a poet to sing their songs; but this is not strange, for literature itself is an expression of social thought and feeling, and partakes of the character of its makers and its readers. For many years the reading of books was the luxury of the few rather than the necessity of the many; but even then society as a whole was influenced by literature, and not merely a small section of it, though the lower classes were affected only indirectly through the upper classes. Through whatever medium that influence may formerly have passed it is certain that for at least a century and a half literature has had an appreciable effect upon social life and action.

It is desirable to emphasize, even at the risk of repetition, the important fact that literature, though it may present only the life of a past epoch, is a power in the development of society, because it appeals to the emotional as well as to the intellectual. A cold and vulgar rationalism affects to despise emotion as an incentive to action, and maintains that in a developed society reason is everywhere and always dominant. Whether that type of society would represent a progress forward or backward, we may leave to others to discuss. As a matter of fact, in the individual living in the society of today feeling is fundamental. Perhaps it is not true, as Beaconsfield declared, that the world is ruled by sentiment, but there is so much of truth in it that no one can afford to disregard it who is constructing a philosophy of life that is to be of any practical worth. It is not enough for people to know of an injustice which they have the power to rectify. They must *feel* it before they will leave their accustomed routine to demand, with an emphasis that means anything, that that injustice be done away. That the demand must be fortified by fact and approved by reason no one would deny; but emotion is the spark that sets reason on fire and makes it efficient in the destruction of evil. There must be "noble ground for noble emotions;" but neither the "noble ground" nor the "noble emotion" can be spared, if efficient action is to be secured. There are not a few who must be made to feel keenly before they will think deeply. To neglect either one of these two great factors in social progress would be to put a part for the whole.

Secondly, literature does much to bring the society of its own day to self-consciousness. Nearly all that has been said of the results of the study of the past by writers of literature applies with equal force to the study of the present. Poets and novelists observe carefully the social phenomena of their own day; separate the transient from the permanent; give beautiful and forceful expression to principles of lasting value;

show the tendencies of thought and action, the social significance of customs and institutions; reveal wrongs and abuses; voice the otherwise unspoken desires and aspirations of all classes from the highest to the socially submerged; and appeal to the emotions and intellects of those who ought to lead the way to social betterment. One of the primary requisites for the writer is an imagination which will enable him to place himself in the midst of situations which he has conceived, not merely as a cool and calculating observer, but as an active and sympathetic participant. He must have the ability to enter into the characters he portrays, the scenes he pictures, the conditions he describes. Thus to him even the past becomes present, because for the time being his world is the thought-world. In imagination he sees his visions and dreams his dreams. He thinks the thoughts of those who lived in a past time, feels what they felt, endures their wrongs, is inspired by their hopes and depressed by their woes. Such an one writes of the past with the vividness and sympathy and power of the present, because to him the past is the present, and he writes of what he feels and knows.

If it be said that this imaginative quality detracts from the value of literature for the student of society, we should remember that the writer must first study in most careful detail the period of which he writes before he can safely venture to put pen to paper. He cannot neglect a single available source of information concerning the period in question without danger of injury to the artistic product. He must be the close and critical student before he can be the portrayer of life. M. Gevaert declares that creation in art is memory modified by personality. If the artist were not first a discoverer, he would have nothing to remember and vivify by the power of his personality. His merit is that he gives reality and life to that which before was vague, unreal, and dead. No one can understand the past who does not possess and use imagination.

But imagination is almost as essential to the understanding and representation of the present as of the past. To enter into the lives of others is a part of the task of the one who writes of his own day. He must thoroughly understand the external conditions as well as the thoughts, feelings, and desires of those for whom he attempts to speak. He can gain this result only by imagination. To look upon houses and fields and persons and classes no more gives an understanding of the inner lives of the people than the sight of the crust of Vesuvius tells of the terrific fires that are raging in its heart. To be sure, it is not a fool's task to observe carefully and describe accurately the external conditions of life. But only the " seer " can discern, and only the genuine artist can portray, the " thoughts which do often lie too deep for tears," and which are, after all, the determining factors in a social condition. Sight is not so rare as insight.

This sympathetic insight into the heart of an age, a people, a class, is an indispensable prerequisite to the one who would aid in the task of bringing an epoch to self-consciousness. No one can interpret anything of which he has not a sympathetic understanding. Even if this were possible, people would be very slow to accept an interpretation of their inner life that was offered by a cynic or an unsympathetic critic.

Interpretation, if it be truthful involves the revelation of certain facts and conditions which reflect discredit upon the people. The knowledge of these things is always unwelcome. The truthfulness of the revelation is usually at first emphatically denied, and the denial is frequently perfectly sincere. The people were ignorant of certain conditions which actually existed, and so were unconscious of any criminal negligence on their own part in permitting the continuance of evils which they might have investigated and exterminated. They were unaware that their own ways of thinking and feeling about certain social evils were the result of traditions and conventions which were sanctioned by usage rather than by justice and right. They failed to see that these thoughts and feelings are a psychical inheritance from the past, are out of harmony with the latest and best developments of their own age, and are a direct contradiction to much that is highest and best in their own standards of thought and life.

The possibility of the dwelling together of these contradictions in the same mind without any seeming recognition that they are contradictions, is one of the curious facts of psychology. There are more than isolated examples of men who under the roof of the church repeat the Golden Rule with pious fervor, and in the market do unto others exactly what they do not wish others to do unto them. Many such men do not see any real inconsistency between the repetition of the formula and their practices in business. When such a man sees in *David Harum* the time-honored adage transposed to read, " Do unto the other feller the way he'd like to do unto you, and do it fust," he is startled into the suspicion that some one has been prying into his private affairs. So common is this harmonious cohabitation of contradictions in the same mind that when a man is found, like Jonathan Edwards, who is actually consistent, we are shocked. Many theologians of his time declared that God is just and good, and yet were horrified that so large a portion of the race were foreordained to eternal damnation by this same good God. Edwards saw that whatever a good God decrees must be good, and, as Professor W. L. Phelps says, not only swallowed the whole thing, but actually declared it tasted good. Edwards rejoiced in the damnation of the wicked because it was the work of a good God, and must therefore in itself be good.

Edwards was a writer of literature as well as a powerful preacher, and his, to us, musty and sulphurous theology helped to bring the people of his day to self-consciousness. When thoughts and beliefs, emotions and aspirations, are objectified in literature, men are compelled to see the relations of part to part as never before, to harmonize contradictions, and to judge of particular beliefs and feelings as right or wrong, injurious or helpful, to individuals and to groups. When the inner life of a people is visualized in literature, the program followed out is frequently something like this: first an indignant and wholesale denial of the truth of the representation; then a suspicion on the part of the more enlightened that there may be a grain of truth in all the chaff of exaggeration and misrepresentation; then a careful investigation to ascertain how much is true and how much false; then the diffusion of the knowledge of facts gained by investigation; then

the adoption of reforms to remedy the evils discovered.

Besides bringing those who had become dull
and torpid, by reason of their long exclusion
from opportunities of self-development, to a consciousness of the fact that they are enduring
oppression which neither individuals nor systems
have any right to put upon them; besides arousing people in general to a sympathetic appreciation of the higher ambitions and possibilities of
those who are the victims of injustice sanctioned
only by ignorance, foolish traditions, and unwarranted customs; besides all this, literature acts as
a sort of safety-valve for the feelings of indigna-
tion and wrath, the sense of injustice and wrong,
which, if they did not find this outlet, might
manifest themselves in ways more violent and
dangerous.   To be sure, this is a two-edged
sword and may cut in either direction.   Literature may aid in stirring up rebellion and revolution as well as in quelling them.   To determine
the exact influence of literature in any particular
case, many factors would have to be taken into
account, which cannot be specially considered
here, such as: the form and spirit of the literary
product; the direct accessibility of the literature
to those who feel that they are suffering the
wrong which ought to be redressed; the tempera-
ment, intelligence, self-restraint, and social or-

ganization of the wronged; the attitude assumed by those who, rightly or wrongly, are supposed to be responsible for the oppression, and who would profit socially or financially by its continuance.

All these factors have an important bearing upon the subject; but the point to which we wish to give special emphasis here is the hope and optimism inspired in those who feel that they have suffered injury at the hands of society or of another class. This hopefulness arises from a consciousness that others know of the wrong endured and feel it as a wrong. There is ground then for the belief that redress is on the way. To suffer alone without the sympathy of others, from causes for which the sufferer is not responsible, is a dangerous thing for an individual or a class. When once a man feels that every man's hand is against him, it is usually only a matter of time when his hand will be against every man.

This perhaps is even more true of a group than of an individual, because of that mysterious influence which impels the crowd to do what would not be done by individuals acting separately. Feeling is inflamed and angrily expressed in a crowd. The individual takes a sober second thought and more rational measures to secure the result which he desires. To give to those who are suffering from real or im-

agined oppression assurance of sympathy and
brotherhood, to inspire them with the hope that
here in this present world, and with as little delay as possible, their wrongs .will be redressed
and their rights to the best things of life will
be fully recognized, this is to transform the mob
into the debating society which has for its object to discover social truth, or into the peaceable
union working for the ends of justice by legal
and rational means. This destroys the material
out of which mobs and riots and revolutions are
made. To secure this end literature, though
not the sole, is a very efficient agent.

Thirdly, literature has a distinct value as an
aid to social progress because of its embodiment
of the highest individual and social ideals. The
power of an ideal over an individual or a race
is unmeasured and unmeasurable. Ideals grow
and change with the change and growth of those
by whom they are formed and cherished. The
nation whose ideal has been industrial may come
to possess the ideal of conquest and empire, and
there is not a village or hamlet within her borders that will not feel the influence of the
change. James Lane Allen has a passage upon
the two different kinds of ideals which is worth
quoting here. He says:

Ideals are of two kinds. There are those that corre-
spond to our highest sense of perfection. . . . They are

not useless because unattainable. . . . . What are they like — ideals such as these? They are like lighthouses. But lighthouses are not made to live in; neither can we live in such ideals. I suppose they are meant to shine on us from afar, when the sea of our life is dark and stormy, perhaps to remind us of a haven of hope, as we drift or sink in shipwreck. . . . . But there are ideals of another sort. . . . . As we advance into life, out of larger experience of the world and of ourselves are unfolded the ideals of what will be possible to us if we make the best use of the world and of ourselves, taken as we are. Let these be as high as they may, they will always be lower than those others which are perhaps veiled intimations of our immortality. . . . . It is these that are to burn for us, not like lighthouses in the distance, but like candles in our hands. . . . . By degrees the comforting light of what you may actually do and be in an imperfect world will shine close to you and all around you, more and more. It is this that will lead you, never to perfection, but always toward it.[5]

Both of these kinds of ideals are given in literature, because both are efficient in life. It would be useless to speculate as to which is the more powerful in influencing thought and action, for both are necessary. Candles are of greatest service in revealing the nearest dangers, but the lighthouse sends out the beams which promise infinite progress and inspire in the heart of the mariner an infinite hope. Ideals are, after all, the product of the study of the past and present,

[5] *The Choir Invisible,* pp. 312–14.

modified by the dominant intentions and the sublimest visions of a personality.   It is because of
this change in ideals, corresponding to the change
in idealists, that poetry and story-telling are a
perpetual necessity.   Thus it is that every age
must have its own novelists and poets to express
its vision of the candle and of the lighthouse.
This seems to us a great lack of economy.   We
see no reason, in the nature of things, why
Homer might not have pictured the ideals of perfection once for all, and left the poets of the
subsequent ages free to sing of other themes.
But nature, everywhere wasteful, is as spend-
thrift of poets as of seeds and flowers.   Every
age has its own candle, showing the obstacles
and the beauties which are nearest.   These are
always different from those which surrounded
any preceding period.   It has also its own pencil
of lighthouse rays which are a little brighter and
more luminous than any that reached a former
age.   " Every fall of the race is a fall upward,"
and brings it a little nearer the great source of
its light.   Even the pessimist, who believes that
all progress is negative, and therefore not progress at all, but retrogression, would still admit
that every epoch must have its own literature, if
its own intellectual, emotional, and social life
is to find adequate expression.   The individ-
uality of every period is shown in its ideals more,

perhaps, than in anything else, and nowhere are those ideals more fully and definitely expressed than in literature.

It is doubtless a truism that ideals are the dominant, transforming power in the individual and in society. The recognition of the fact is, however, more theoretical than practical. If this were the place to call attention to the terrible need of the practical application of some of the things we claim to know so well, we might remind ourselves that often the essential difference between the criminal and the law-abiding citizen is a difference in ideals. The fifteen-year-old boy in the Chicago slums aspires to be a " tough " because the men he sees and knows, and those of whom he reads in his " three-for-a-nickel " library, have created in him an ideal of manhood to which the criminal alone corresponds. That we take little practical recognition of this, which we are almost ready to call a truism, is evidenced by the fact that we still allow, and by our negligence encourage, the formation of these ideals by permitting the sale of journalistic trash, and compelling the young offender to associate with desperate and hardened criminals in jails and penitentiaries. It is not exaggeration to say that he is a real benefactor to the world who hammers in a few such things that everybody knows. Among these few things are the

Ten Commandments, the " ethical chestnuts " of
Dr. Parkhurst. " To say a thing," says Goethe,
" that everybody else has said before, as quietly
as if nobody had ever said it, *that* is originality.
The great merit of the old painters was that they
did not try to be original."   Goethe's originality
is in itself an ideal of genuine social value.

But not only does literature give expression to
the individual and social ideals of the time.   It
is also one of the forces which help to create the
dominant ideals of society.   Too much stress
must not be laid upon this part of the subject.
Nothing must obscure the truth that always the
primary purpose of literature is representation,
rather than creation, of life and ideals.   The
poets especially give to us the highest ideals of
their day, and to the average man these seem
to be the creation of the poet, when in reality
they are only faithful pictures of the actual visions of the purest and noblest souls.   Everyone
recognizes that a man sees only what he is prepared to see, and if the poets see the highest
ideals in man and in society, and give to these a
beautiful expression, they are doing much to
make the ideals themselves a transforming power
in the social world.   By such a revelation they
arouse in the minds of men a desire to attain the
ideals portrayed, and this is a necessary first step
to the actual attainment.   To adapt the definition

of Gevaert to our purpose, we may say that the poetic creation of ideals is really representation modified by the personality of the poet.

It is to be expected that the soul that is clear-visioned enough to see these highest ideals for the individual and the race, will also be peculiarly sensitive to all the tendencies and influences which aid in their attainment or which tend to their obscuration. We have already said sufficient upon the subject of the relation of literature to these influences and tendencies in speaking of the literary study of the past and the present. The only point to which special attention need here be called is the relation of these tendencies and influences to the actual attainment of the ideals portrayed. This is really only a specific application of the principles before stated. The ideals form the standard by which the influences and tendencies are judged. Whatever brings the individual and the race nearer the cherished ideals is approved; whatever retards the progress in this direction is condemned. The work is therefore, in this aspect of it, partly destructive and partly constructive. The constructive work is the more positive and aggressive. The destructive work is as often accomplished by neglect, scorn, or refusal to approve, as by positive condemnation.

No one who has thought upon the subject can

have failed to have noticed the chasm between
the ideals presented by literature and the actual
conditions at any particular time. We are compelled to ask: How can this chasm be bridged?
To this question literature gives no satisfactory
answer. That the chasm is deep and wide there
can be no doubt, but in our difficulty we must go
to someone other than the poet or novelist for
help. Here we find one of the undoubted limitations of the usefulness of literature to the practical worker for the betterment of society. While
the crowd is wallowing in the mire, the poet cries:
" I will lift up mine eyes unto the mountains."
That is a cry of confidence and hope and cheer.
It gives strength and courage for effort, but, unfortunately, it does not lift the wallowing herd
to the summit upon which the poet has fixed his
gaze. It may be that it is for this reason that
literature has been almost wholly disregarded as
an agency for social service. Because it has not
constructed a complete social philosophy, offered
immediate solutions for all the vexed problems of
society, and constructed programs warranted to
usher in a millennium on schedule time; because
it has not done these things, it has been ignored,
almost as if it had done nothing of social importance. While programs are the order of the
day, it is certainly true that literature has no
special claim for conspicuous notice. But, on

the other hand, it is as certainly true that literature has rendered a much more efficient and valuable service, as we have tried to show. To be
sure, some makers of literature have tried their
hands at making programs, but never with eminent success, and usually with conspicuous failure.
Their failures have been no worse, perhaps, than
those of many others who have made similar attempts; but this is cold comfort. The simple
fact is that poets and novelists do not know how
to construct a practical social program, and the
wisest of them have understood this, and, following the advice of Carlyle, have minded their
own business. Those who have been less wise
have made the attempt, and have demonstrated
by their failures their inability to do successfully
what they have so boldly attempted.

But if Arnold was right when he wrote that
our urgent need now is " to lay in a stock of light
for our difficulties; " [6] if Miss Scudder is right in
saying that " the race will never abandon an ideal
once realized, but will raise all to its level," [7] then
literature must be recognized as one of the important factors contributing to social progress;
for it does add to our " stock of light," and it
does aid in establishing and realizing individual
and social ideals which the race will never aban-

[6] *Culture and Anarchy,* chap. 2.
[7] *Social Ideals,* p. 273.

don until all rise to their level.   Miss Scudder
continues: " First to establish a lofty standard;
then, through the action of the state, to realize
conditions in which the free upward-striving. instinct of men may make that standard universal
— such is the order of social evolution." [8]   It
is perhaps largely because literature has to do
with the earlier stages of the process of social
evolution rather than the later that its greatest
contributions to individual and race-progress
have been all but universally ignored.   The publication of books like Miss Scudder's *Social Ideals
in English Letters* and of Kuno Francke's *Social
Forces in German Literature* indicates that we
are about to give a tardy recognition to literature
as a factor in social evolution.   Yet these books
are more significant for what they prophesy than
for what they accomplish.

III

As to the methods employed by literature in
accomplishing the results enumerated but little
need be said.   As a general characterization of
literature we may quote the words of the *Standard Dictionary,* omitting the explantory paren-
theses:

Literature, in its narrowest and strictest sense, belongs to the sphere of high art, and embodies thought

[8] *Loc. cit.*

that is power-giving, or inspiring and elevating, rather than merely knowledge-giving; catholic, or of interest to man as man; æsthetic in its tone and style; and shaped by the creative imagination, or power of artistic construction.

Having this general explanation in mind, we may say that the methods employed by literature in rendering this unconscious social service may be classified under two general heads:

1. Simple statements of facts, physical or psychical, are rarely ranked as literary products, though simplicity is one of the essentials of great art. Some essays, however, which are generally classed as literature consist almost wholly of such declarations. Simple statements of facts may be " power-giving " or inspiring, if the facts are rightly chosen and skilfully arranged.

2. The imaginative presentation of conditions, needs, and ideals is an effective method of calling attention to abuses which ought to be abolished. Here physical, psychical, and social facts become tools for the use of the imagination in creative art. The most important means used to make this imaginative presentation effective are these: (a) By the use of rhythm, literature gains an added power over certain minds. The degree of susceptibility to impression by rhythmical forms varies greatly in different persons; sometimes also in the same person at different

periods of life. (*b*) By the use of love in its
romantic forms, literature creates and maintains
interest in characters, classes, and periods. The
relation of this to the development of the family
has peculiar importance to the student of society.
(*c*) Satire has been used effectively by poets and
novelists as a sting for those guilty of allowing
the continuance of social evils, and as a spur to
social remedial action. (*d*) By his appeals to
compassion and sympathy, the writer of literature
arouses the emotions, and thus gives needful
stimulus for the correction of errors and the improvement of conditions.

If we say, in conclusion, that literature, viewed
from the standpoint of sociology, can never be
allowed the watchword " art for art's sake "
without vigorous protest, we are saying no more
than many of the best students of literature are
saying. In fact, that much-vaunted formula, to
the layman, seems to be either meaningless or
absolutely false. In a world of human beings
there is and can be no art that is unrelated to
man. Man is the artist, and man is the judge of
that which is created. To be sure, art must be
sincere and true; but this only means that its
appeal must be to the higher and not to the lower
man. Thus, instead of " art for art's sake," we
have the truer and more meaningful formula
" art for man's sake." If we understand by the

term "man" the highest and divinest man, the watchword is as good for literature as it is for sociology; for we have shown that the service of literature to sociology is dependent upon the maintenance of the highest artistic standards. Sociology asks of literature, not a disquisition upon the nature and function of the social organism, but a faithful, sympathetic, artistic, vital portrayal of the physical, intellectual, emotional, and moral life of persons, classes, and periods.

Most of the best work that literature has done for society cannot be put into figures, or given a definite and accurate statement, because this work is fundamental and spiritual. It is only the coarser, cruder, less vital, and less important facts and forces of life that lend themselves to the uses of the gauger and the statistician. The scales have not yet been invented by which we can measure the social service rendered to the world by Dante, in becoming the interpreter of the Middle Ages; in transforming the conception of love from a sensual appetite into a spiritual and ideal passion; in becoming the herald of a new era of liberty, purity, and service in the church. The value to the race of the valiant championship of civil and religious liberty by John Milton in prose and verse is utterly beyond computation. Mrs. Browning's "Cry of the Children" was based upon Horne's report of the condition of mines and factories, and hastened an act of Parliament restricting the employment of children of tender years. Of so much we are morally certain; but how great was the influence of this poem in securing this act of Parliament no one can tell, for other forces were also working toward the same end. When President Lincoln was introduced to Mrs. H. B. Stowe in Washington in 1863, he said: " Is this the little woman who caused the war? " The words must not be taken too literally, of course; but there is in them a statesman's recognition of the influence exerted by one maker of literature, in bringing about social changes of the greatest significance.

If we ask for the difference between the social service rendered by poetry and that rendered by fiction, we find no complete and satisfactory answer. No statement could be made to which there would not be so many exceptions as to make the result seem almost valueless. It has been said that the novel is the most effective weapon of satire, and that poetry is the best medium for the presentation of ideals. As a general characterization, this may be allowed to stand, though everyone thinks at once of prose that is more poetic than poetry, and of poetry more prosaic than prose. Remembering that there are idealistic novels and satirical poems, we may take the general statement for what it is worth. Our concern being especially with poetry, it is natural and desirable that particular attention be given to those phases of social service for which poetry is conspicuous. If " a noble standard of life is the first need of social evolution," [9] poetry has had a great opportunity of meeting a primary social need by revealing the highest possibilities of man as man, and thus helping to establish that " noble standard." This opportunity has not passed unimproved.

" Poetry holds at all times the truth of the future," [10] and thus heralds the dawn of the ever-new day and leads the way. So long a time frequently elapses between the enunciation of a truth and its universal acceptance; so many voices have to take up the cry of the herald before it reaches the utmost bounds of the land; so many auxiliary influences are frequently called into play to aid in the establishment of a truth that has already been fearlessly proclaimed, that often the poet, the first discoverer, is shouted down by the noisy cries of those who have taken the message from his lips. Often the poet,

> The first discoverer starves — his followers, all
> Flower into fortune. [11]

[9] *Social Ideals,* p. 273.
[10] *Ibid.,* p. 232.
[11] Tennyson, " Columbus," p. 527.

" The true Sovereign of the world," says Carlyle, " who molds the world, like soft wax, according to his pleasure, is he who lovingly *sees* into the world; the inspired Thinker whom in these days we name Poet." [12]

[12] *Miscellaneous Essays,* Vol. I, p. 152.

CHAPTER II

SOCIAL CONDITIONS IN ENGLAND IN THE TIME OF TENNYSON

We are now to study somewhat in detail the application of the principles enunciated in the preceding chapter to the work of Alfred Tennyson. The poems of Tennyson would certainly not be selected first, if we were to choose volumes of nineteenth-century poetry in the order of their social significance; and some have gone so far as to say that the poems of the great laureate have no social importance at all. That this latter view is completely mistaken it will not, I think, be difficult to show.

Because Tennyson was supremely the artist of his century, and one of the greatest artists of any century, the social value of his work as the mirror of his age has been ignored or positively denied; but we have seen that the social value of a literary product is not opposed to, but, in a sense, is dependent upon, its artistic quality. Artistic perfection does not of itself give assurance that any work will be of social service; but if a novel or poem which might otherwise possess a social value lacks the artistic quality, its use-fulness is thereby destroyed or rendered transient. With this view of the artist's place in society, Tennyson becomes exceedingly interesting to the student of sociology. He did not formulate a schedule of social movements; but we are learn-ing that the quest for novel social theories and startling programs is more than a weariness to the flesh; for, even when successful, the theories and programs discovered are found to be of lit-tle practical value.

Before entering upon a study of the poems themselves, however, we need to understand as clearly as possible the social world in which Ten-nyson began his work. We may fix upon 1830 as the date of the beginning of his life-labors, the year in which he published *Poems, Chiefly Lyrical*. His only publications which preceded this volume were *Poems by Two Brothers*, by Charles and Alfred Tennyson in 1827, and *Tim-buctoo*, a poem which obtained the chancellor's medal at the Cambridge commencement in 1829. Alfred Tennyson was between fifteen and seven-teen years of age when his contributions to the volume *Poems by Two Brothers* were written, and nineteen or twenty when the prize poem was prepared for his Cambridge audience. These verses have little significance for our purpose. Indeed, he wrote of himself in 1890: " I suppose I was nearer thirty than twenty before I was anything of an artist." [1]   It is with the poetry of Tennyson after he became a master-workman that we are especially concerned, and the volumes of 1830 and 1832 are not without genuine artistic quality.

What were the social conditions existing in England in the nineteenth century, or during that part of it in which Tennyson lived?   Someone has said that the nineteenth century began in 1789, and if we accept the statement, we shall have over a hundred years to summarize in one brief chapter.   It is evident that we can only glance at the prominent features of a period which contains much that is worthy of being studied in detail.   Professor Charles Zueblin gives five social characteristics of the seventeenth and eighteenth centuries: (1) political reform, (2) extension of commerce, (3) industrial revolution, (4) liberty of the press, and (5) Wesleyan revival.   The industrial revolution is the central fact in the eighteenth century.   It is one of those large movements that cannot be said to have begun in a specified year, but which may be placed roughly at the close of the eighteenth century.   Important inventions had been made, the full significance of which no one at the time could have appreciated.   The spinning-frame,

[1] *Memoir*, Vol. I, p. 12.

the spinning-mule, the power-loom, and the cotton-gin, called into being in the latter half of the eighteenth century were destined to work marvelous changes in the life of the people. The motive power of steam had been discovered, and early prophesied some of the transformations which have since proved of immense economic value.

With the altered conditions brought about by these wonderful inventions we are familiar, because they have continued down to the present time. Every decade brings changes, but the later years have only extended and developed the methods and the machinery which first made applicable the term " industrial revolution." It is necessary for us to remember that up to the middle of the eighteenth century practically all manufactures were carried on by hand. Factories were almost unknown. Few, if any, large towns were devoted to any one trade. The manufacturer was often the farmer, who employed part of his time in the pursuit of agriculture and part in weaving cloth in his own house. The cottage of the laborer was almost the only factory. The old-fashioned spinning-wheel and the hand-loom were the ordinary instruments of production. Steam power was unknown, and so little coal was mined as to be of trifling importance in the solution of the problem of fuel.

When Tennyson began his work in 1830, these conditions were greatly changed. Steam was then being applied to almost every industry, new machines had been invented, coal was being mined in large quantities, the means of transportation had been vastly improved. The steamship had been created, and heralded the advent of the railroad train. Population had increased, and began to be concentrated in large towns given over to manufactures of various sorts.

The agitation for political changes became pronounced in this period, though much of the desired legislation was not secured until later. The Reform Bill was passed in 1832. Not until that year did the new factory workers receive their rightful share in the government, and the agricultural population obtain a more adequate representation. With the passing of that bill the power of the land-owning class was severely curtailed, and democracy gained a new and important victory.[2] The Corn Laws were not repealed until 1846.

In 1815 Napoleon received his crushing defeat at Waterloo at the hands of the Duke of Wellington. The years of war preceding that

[2] See Gibbins, *The English People in the Nineteenth Century*, p. 26.

battle had cost the nation millions of pounds. The wealth acquired by the development of industry and commerce was in one sense quite as essential to the victory of England as the prowess of her soldiers.   When at last peace was declared and the nation had time to consider the condition of its own people, the working classes were suffering from high prices of food, low wages, and high taxes.   In fact, the whole country was groaning under the overwhelming load of taxation, while money was so scarce that for twenty years preceding 1819 the Bank of England had not gold enough to cash its own notes.[3]

Those who suffered most keenly as a result of these conditions were naturally the poor. They had no reserve fund upon which to draw. They were almost entirely dependent for their livelihood upon the product of their daily toil. The men who had worked only by hand found themselves without employment, because the new machines tended by women or children were doing the work the men had been accustomed to do, and were doing it faster and better than they could do it.   Workmen became dependent upon capitalist employers, and a competition before unknown became a powerful factor in industry and commerce.

The moral and physical conditions of the fac-

[3] Gibbins, *op. cit.*, p. 2.

tory workers were often wretched. Persons of all ages and both sexes were crowded into large factories, with no arrangements for the preservation of health, morality, comfort, or decency. Poverty seemed to compel as sad conditions in the home as in the factory. In Manchester one-tenth of the total population lived in cellars, which were often flooded with stagnating filth. In these miserable holes entire families lived crowded together, sleeping on the damp and filthy floors, through which moisture was continually oozing up sending out disgusting odors. The children from such homes as these and from the poorhouses were employed in the factories as veritable slaves. To read the record of the cruel, inhuman, devilish treatment of these children, of their abuse and overwork, makes the blood run hot. It was mentioned in Parliament in 1815 that children were actually bought and sold by employers as if they were slaves; but who cared? [4]

We cannot wonder that during the years in which the changes were taking place pauperism greatly increased. The industrial revolution, war, agricultural and manufacturing failures and losses, forced many of the poorest people out of the self-supporting class and into the ranks of the dependent. Under the provision of the Corn

[4] *Ibid.*, p. 3.

Laws, passed in 1815 and re-enacted at later dates, foreign corn could not be imported till English wheat was almost at famine price. P. A. Graham [5] quotes the testimony of a man who was obliged to live on raw turnips or boiled nettles, because unable to pay the high price demanded for bread. Even Queen Victoria wrote as late as 1847: " The price of bread is so high that we have been obliged to reduce every one to a pound a day, and only secondary flour to be used in the royal kitchen." If royalty was thus stinted, the condition of the poor may perhaps be imagined.[6]

Relief of some sort was imperatively demanded. Since 1796 outdoor relief had been given to laborers, whether able-bodied or not: The pernicious policy of supplementing wages by poor-rates was commonly followed. To this folly was added that of giving relief according to the number of children in a family, thus encouraging profligacy and improvident marriages.

By these means pauperism, so far from being checked, was actually encouraged. In 1818 the poor-rate had increased to 13 s. 3 d. per head. While the condition of the poor was thus going from bad to worse, England's ambition for commercial supremacy was steadily growing. France

[5] *The Victorian Era,* p. 26.
[6] Gibbins, *op. cit.,* p. 36.

was in this field a formidable rival, and this fact did not tend to increase the friendship of the two nations.   Napoleon showed that he was determined to make France the leading country in commerce, not only of Europe, but of the world. This purpose in the great Corsican was a trumpet-call to Britain to gird herself for battle in the markets of the world as well as upon the field of war.

The day of cottage factories was past.   Manufacturing industries developed, merchants became more enterprising and daring, and consequently foreign trade increased in variety and in value. The colonies which we now know as the United States had been lost, but many others remained, including such important sources of trade as Canada and India.   Yet as late as 1820 the value of England's foreign and colonial imports was only about thirty-two million pounds sterling, and the imports and exports combined were only seventy-nine millions; while in the three years preceding 1840 the average of imports rose to fifty-six millions, and the total imports and exports to one hundred and fifteen millions.   In the twenty years following 1840 the increase in foreign and colonial trade was still more remarkable.

It was not until 1836 that the heavy tax of four pence on each newspaper was so reduced as

to cease to be prohibitive for a large portion of
the population.   About the same time the duty
on paper was diminished.   This meant much to
the poor people of England and to all lovers of
cheap literature.   In 1837 Mr. Rowland Hill
proposed to abolish all existing rates of postage,
and to substitute therefor a uniform rate of one
penny, irrespective of distance, with prepayment
by means of stamps.   This suggestion, which at
first aroused a storm of opposition, was adopted
by Parliament in 1839.

The agitation for the removal of the religious
disabilities grew warm in the early years of the
century.   Catholics were not allowed to sit in
Parliament or hold any public office.   William
Pitt attempted to change these unfair conditions
in 1801, but without success.   In 1810 Grattan
repeated the effort of Pitt, and with the same
result.   Partial success came in 1817, when, by
the passage of the Military and Naval Officers'
Oath Bill, all ranks of the army and navy were
opened to Catholics and Dissenters.   In 1823
the Catholic Association, a large and influential
society, was called into being to aid in the work
of Catholic emancipation.   Two years later Parliament passed an act to dissolve the association
as a dangerous body.   In 1828 Daniel O'Connell, the eloquent advocate of freedom and tolera-
tion, was elected to Parliament for County Clare,

but, being a Roman Catholic, he could not take his seat. This precipitated a crisis, and in 1829, in spite of fierce opposition, a bill was passed by both houses which opened Parliament to Roman Catholics. The restrictions upon Protestant Dissenters had been removed the year before, so that when Tennyson published his *Poems, Chiefly Lyrical* very few persons in England were at political disadvantage because of their religious views.

Besides the changes already enumerated, there were other important events and transformations that took place during the life of the poet. Some of these are definitely referred to in the poems, some are reflected in his verses only in spirit and not mentioned by name, while concerning others he is absolutely silent. Each method of treating great facts and movements has its own significance. " Silence is vocal, if we listen well."

In the industrial world the changes were perhaps most marked and most prophetic of the " age that is to be." In 1830 the first co-operative farm was founded, followed fourteen years later by the organization of the Rochdale Equitable Pioneers. In 1832 genuine trades unions were formed. A year afterward factory inspectors were appointed. In 1842 women and children were prohibited from working in underground galleries. Five and eight years later

Sadler, Oastler, and the Earl of Shaftesbury suc-
ceeded in securing legislation for the further pro-
tection of women and children employed in mines
and factories.   In 1862 devices for the safety
and ventilation of mines were introduced.   In
1870 payment in " truck " was abolished.   In
1889 the dockers' strike showed to the world the
great power of united labor.   The Chartist in-
surrection took place as far back as 1839, and
opened the eyes of many to the possible peril
arising from the wrath of the oppressed when
once aroused.   The formation of the Electric
Telegraph Company in 1846, and the rapid extension of railways in the fifteen years succeed-
ing, together with the ever-increasing activity of
the press, served to unify the people of the realm
in a remarkable degree.

In politics also there were social signs of the
times.   The great event of the early part of the
period of which we are thinking was, of course,
the passage of the Reform Bill in 1832.   In 1833
the negroes were emancipated, and the Quakers
were admitted to Parliament.   In 1848 the first
public-health act was passed.   In 1850 the funds
of the Friendly Societies were legally protected.
Three years later the United Kingdom alliance
was formed to suppress the liquor traffic.   In
1857 representative government was given some
of the Australian colonies, and Jews were ad-

mitted to Parliament.   In 1860 protective duties
were completely abolished, and the Radicals
secured the freedom of the press.   In 1868 the
Dominion of Canada was formed.   A short time
afterward women were given votes in municipal
elections and allowed to vote for school boards.
In 1873 the " settlement idea " had its inception.
Two years later the sanitary code was consoli-
dated.   In 1883 the Fabian Society was formed.
In 1884 Englishmen could make the proud boast
that no civil disabilities were attached to any class
of British subjects.   In 1891 the London County
Council was formed, and lords and laborers sat in
one body.   So rapid was the growth of the
democratic idea in Albion's realm.

There is also some special legislation that is
worthy of note, aside from the factory acts already mentioned.   In 1843 imprisonment for
debt was abolished in all cases except for fraud.
The repeal of the Corn Laws in 1846 has already been cited.   Various other acts, such as
the " Baths and Wash Houses Act," " Free Libraries Act," " Municipal Reform Act," " Education Act," and the " Housing of the Working
Classes Act," all showed that the needs of the
people were being recognized and met by the law
of the land.

The cause of education in the realm also
showed a decided, if not a thoroughly satisfac-

tory, advance. In 1833 the government took charge of the education of the poor. In 1839 the first inspectors of schools were appointed, and a special department was created to supervise the work. About 1850 the newspapers were multiplying and coming to positions of great power. In 1851 there were 159 newspapers in London alone. In 1853 there were grants made for building schools in poor places. In 1860 Rev. F. D. Maurice established his " Workingmen's College " in London. Seven years later the university-extension movement was started in Cambridge. In 1870 the voluntary schools were supplemented by board schools, and the religious conditions for school attendance were abolished. The right of women to higher and professional education was so far accorded that in 1876 every recognized medical body was authorized to open its doors to women. Two years later the supplementary charter granted to the University of London enabled it to open all its degrees to women. In 1880 there began an era of marked improvement in schools, which continued up to and after the death of Tennyson. This was a source of great comfort and hope to the poet, who considered education one of the most efficient means of remedying social disorders.

During this period there were indications of new interest in the æsthetic side of life. As early as 1843 a number of schools of design had entered upon successful careers.   In six or seven years the pre-Raphaelite movement had begun. In 1851 the first great exhibition was held.   In a few years various Ruskin societies were formed. In 1868 William Morris started the "Kelmscott Press," and about ten years later began his lectures on art.

In the ecclesiastical world there was also movement and change.   In 1834 there was the Wesleyan secession, which resulted in giving much more influence to the laity.   Partly because of this, perhaps, there was, two years later, a movement toward church reform.   In 1865 the Salvation Army was founded.   It was not until the year before Tennyson's death that the first "labor church" was opened by Trevor in Manchester.

Such movements and events as have been catalogued reveal the spirit of the time in which Tennyson lived.   It will be interesting to notice how he was affected by this spirit, wherein he reflected it, in what way he opposed it, wherein he led and inspired it by giving to it its highest ideal, and in what respect he seemed untouched by it.

NOTE.— This study is based upon the poems as found in the Macmillan & Co.'s one-volume edition published in 1894.   All references to poems are to the pages of this volume.

CHAPTER III

TENNYSON'S IDEA OF MAN

In every theory of society, in every system of social ideals, the fundamental conception is the idea of man. Man puts himself into the family he creates, the government he forms, the industry he conducts. The man of whom the poet conceives an ideal is the being who enters into relations with others of his race in the home, the community, the nation. As he is in himself, so he will be in his relations. As he is in his relations, so will be the society which he forms. Man's duties, responsibilities, destinies, are determined by his nature and possibilities.

Tennyson's words upon this great theme show us how exalted was his ideal of this " creature with the upward gaze." In the opening stanzas of " In Memoriam " he invokes the " strong Son of God, Immortal Love," and declares, " Thou madest man." Mr. Allingham,[1] reporting a conversation of the poet with himself and a friend, quotes these words from Tennyson: " Time is nothing; are we not all a part of Deity? " Yet

[1] *Memoir,* Vol. I, p. 514.

he recognizes man as a distinct personality, who attains his highest nature when most thoroughly himself.

> For a man is not as God,
> But then most Godlike being most a man.[2]

Even the reckless pleasure-hunter of " The Vision of Sin " does not altogether forget that " God's likeness " is " the ground plan " of the man who owns that " Death is King." [3]   Because of this godlike nature he possesses, " man is man and master of his fate." [4]   His relation to Deity is mysterious, but real.   That relationship makes man great today because of what he is to be.

> We feel we are nothing — for all is Thou and in Thee;
> We feel we are something — *that* also has come from Thee;
> We know we are nothing — but Thou wilt help us to be:
> Hallowed be Thy name — Hallelujah.[5]

The measureless capacity of man is explained by the fact that He who made us " Sent the shadow of Himself, the boundless, thro' the human soul." [6]

This does not mean that man as we know him

[2] " Love and Duty," p. 93.
[3] P. 123.
[4] " The Marriage of Geraint," p. 46.
[5] " De Profundis," p. 533.
[6] " Locksley Hall Sixty Years After," p. 566.

is a creature of angelic mold.   He has angel instincts, but he is also akin to the beasts.   Man is
" the piebald miscellany." [7]   When controlled by
anger, he is brother to the wolves.[8]   It is only
the king of fools who would hope or expect to
make men from beasts.[9]   The harmless people
of the newly discovered world took the white
voyagers for " very Gods," but found some of
them " very fiends from Hell." [10]   Even the king
of sacred song declared that men are " insects of
an hour, that hourly work their brother insects
wrong." [11]   The fact that we feel within ourselves " the Powers of Good " and " the Powers
of Ill " may be explained by the presence of
" those about us whom we neither see nor
name." [12]   Harold was right in one sense in saying that " we are all poor earthworms crawling
in this boundless nature," and was himself an
argument in favor of the truth of the statement.[13]
The many characters portrayed in the poems
who bring ruin upon others through passion,
lust, selfishness, malice, hatred, greed, give evi-

[7] " The Princess," p. 198.
[8] " Balin and Balan," p. 377.
[9] " The Last Tournament," p. 449.
[10] " Columbus," p. 528.
[11] " Locksley Hall Sixty Years After," p. 566.
[12] *Ibid.*, p. 567.
[13] " The Voice and the Peak," p. 240.

dence of the poet's knowledge of the possible degradation of a human being. An extract from a letter to Emily Sellwood, dated 1839, corroborates this evidence in the words: " Indeed what matters it how much man knows and does if he keeps not a reverential looking upward? He is only the subtlest beast in the field." [14] It is through the body that man has his most intimate connection with the lower world. Henry, in the drama of " Becket," states what may be taken as Tennyson's own conviction in the words

this beast-body
That God has plunged my soul in.[15]

Recognizing thus frankly the relation of man to the lower animals, studying with scientific care the possible degeneration of the individual through passion, selfishness, sin, he still holds with unwavering firmness that " the highest is the measure of the man." [16] The thought of a man is higher than peak or star.[17] Man is everywhere recognized as nature's last and greatest work.[18] Nor is this conception of the noblest manhood an idle or impossible dream. He

---

[14] *Memoir*, Vol. I, p. 169.

[15] *Poems*, p. 717.

[16] " The Princess," p. 175.

[17] " The Voice and the Peak," p. 240.

[18] " In Memoriam," Canto LVI, p. 261.

pointed to him whom he called "Albert, the Good" as one

> Who reverenced his conscience as his king;
> Whose glory was redressing human wrong;
> Who spake no slander, no, nor listen'd to it;
> Who loved one only and who clave to her.[19]

He was one who possessed

> that gentleness
> Which, when it weds with manhood, makes a man.[20]

The very fact that "we needs must love the highest when we see it." [21] is convincing proof that "the highest human nature is divine." [22] Guinevere's suffering and sin open her eyes to this great truth, and at last she says of Arthur: "Thou are the highest and most human, too." [23] Tennyson portrays many different types of character, but he never allows the reader to forget that God made man in his own image. Even when ruined by his sins, man still shows how great he is. Tennyson's conception of his true worth is indicated by the words of Harold:

> The simple, silent, selfless man
> Is worth a world of tonguesters. [24]

[19] "Dedication of Idylls," p. 308.
[20] "Geraint and Enid," p. 367.
[21] "Guinevere," p. 466.
[22] "Locksley Hall Sixty Years After," p. 568.
[25] "Guinevere," p. 466.
[24] "Harold," Act V, sc. 1, p. 684.

In 1850 he declared that "the real test of a man is not what he knows, but what he is in himself and in his relation to others." [25]   Men may condemn the poet's judgment in speaking such splendid eulogy of Wellington or Havelock or Prince Albert as ideal men, but no one can truly say that he ever forgot the possible divinity of humanity, or neglected to call man to the realization of his great possibilities.

That Tennyson was a firm believer in the freedom of man's will is evidenced by his poems and by his biography. The lines most frequently quoted by him upon this subject are these:

This main miracle that thou art thou
With power on thine own act and on the world. [26]

Miss E. R. Chapman who published *A Companion to In Memoriam* in 1888 quotes the poet's words upon the first stanza of the last section of the great elegy beginning, "O living will, that shalt endure." "I did not mean," said Tennyson, "the divine will, as you say. I meant *will in man* — free will. You know there is free will. It is limited, of course. We are like birds in a cage, but we can hop from perch to perch — till the roof is taken off." [27]   It is not necessary

[25] *Memoir,* Vol. I, p. 318.

[26] *Ibid.,* p. 317.

[27] W. T. Stead, "Character Sketch of Tennyson," *Review of Reviews,* December, 1892, p. 565.

to quote further in support of this statement of
the poet's belief in free will.   Attention is called
to it here because, without this conviction, no one
can consistently believe in the responsibility of
the individual for his own progress and for the
progress of society.

Tennyson's careful study of science naturally
made him a firm adherent of the doctrine of evolution.   He believed every man to be " the heir
of all ages in the foremost files of time." [28]
There is really

> nothing lost to man;
> So that still garden of the souls
> In many a figured leaf enrolls
> The total world since life began.[29]

" Many a million of ages have gone to the making of man;" [30] and these ages of making indicate the value of the product.   Edgar, in " The
Promise of May," [31] speaks of " the man, the
child of evolution."   The countless years of the
past that have gone toward the making of man as
he is today have not completed their task.   Man
still is being made.   Other countless years must
come and go before it can be said that the work
is finished and man is made.

[28] " Locksley Hall,' p. 102.
[29] " In Memoriam," XLIII, p. 258.
[30] " Maud," IV, p. 290.
[31] Act I, p. 784.

Science has in its vast conceptions tended to belittle man. He is lost in the vast cosmic world. The poet recalls us to the truth that the cosmic forces are focused upon the human being. The making of a man by evolution is a slow process, but it gives hope. It works out the beast, and lets the ape and tiger die. The great zones of sculpture that girded the hall of Camelot with their mystic symbols represent four stages in the progress of man.

> In the lowest beasts are slaying men,
> And in the second men are slaying beasts,
> And on the third are warriors, perfect men,
> And on the fourth are men with growing wings.[32]

Now "we are far from the noon of man, there is time for the race to grow." [33] Tennyson's whole philosophy of the onward march of man from the lowest level up to the very summit of his grandest destiny is summed up in " The Making of Man.[34]

Where is one that, born of woman, altogether can escape
From the lower world within him, moods of tiger or of ape?
Man as yet is being made, and ere the crowning Age of ages,
Shall not æon after æon pass and touch him into shape?

[32] " The Holy Grail," p. 422.
[33] " The Dawn," p. 889.
[34] P. 889.

All about him shadows still, but, while the races flower
    and fade,
Prophet-eyes may catch a glory slowly gaining on the
    shade,
Till the peoples all are one, and all their voices blend
    in choric
Hallelujah to the Maker, "It is finished. Man is
    made."

This triumphant message of the poet, philosopher, and idealist prophesies the increasing glory of the individual as well as that of the race. Bishop Westcott wrote that what impressed him most in "In Memoriam" was Tennyson's "splendid faith (in the face of the frankest acknowledgment of every difficulty) in the growing purpose of the sum of life, and in the noble destiny of the individual man as he offers himself for the fulfilment of his little part." [35]

We may now summarize briefly the poet's teaching concerning man, "the social unit." Man is a spirit dwelling in a body. He is a product of evolution and carries in himself the history of the past; yet he is free and

                Strong in will
To strive, to seek, to find and not to yield.[36]

He has aspirations the highest, hopes the grandest, and comes to self-realization largely through

[35] *Memoir,* Vol. I, p. 300.
[36] "Ulysses," p. 96.

action in service of his fellow-men. He possesses reason and is by nature a doubter; yet he is largely influenced by emotions, conventions, nature, environment. He is capable of education, longs for knowledge, purity, love. He is at once capable of the sublimest heroism in the performance of duty, and of most awful degeneration through selfishness and sin. Even failure nobly used may become a stepping-stone in his progress. Faith, obedience, sorrow, suffering, struggle, self-sacrifice, each in its own way ministers to the advancement and highest achievement of the man whose noble destiny is proclaimed by his wondrous possibilities. That destiny is so great that it passes the bounds of earth and finds its perfect fulfilment only in the immortal life. This is the man of whom the poet thinks and sings, the man who puts himself into all his social compacts in family, government, church, and society. This is the unit which remains constant in every computation of social values.

CHAPTER IV

TENNYSON'S IDEA OF THE WORTH AND WORK
OF WOMAN

Tennyson has written so much concerning the place and mission of woman, has pictured so many types of the female character, that a volume would be required to give in detail his study and estimate of the qualities which are regarded as peculiarly feminine. We need not here repeat the questions: Are Tennyson's women real or unreal; are they portrayed with artistic power; do they show as great poetic insight as is revealed in other features of his work? These are interesting and important questions, but they are not ours. We ask: What was Tennyson's conception of the function of woman in the social organism? and seek to find the correct answer to this inquiry.

In King Arthur, Tennyson has given us his ideal man. This beautiful character has no feminine counterpart. Arthur was wedded to Guinevere, who wrought the ruin of the round table. Tennyson has portrayed women of wondrous virtue, beauty, love; but there is not one in

72

all the gallery of his art to whom we can point
and say: "This is the ideal woman." The
noblest women of his song are not the creations
of his imagination, but the product of his pho-
tographic skill. Lilian, Mariana, Madeline,
Oriana, Margaret, are not without attractiveness;
but when he wrote of Victoria, in whom "a
thousand claims to reverence closed   .   .   .
as mother, wife and queen," or of his own mother
as he did in "Isabel,"[1] he wrote with a power
not evinced in the descriptive analyses of the
women of his imagination. The women of his
brain are pretty girls. The noblest women
whom he knew were strong in character and life
and love. In general it is true that the lines
written in earlier manhood portray women whose
attractiveness is transient and external, while his
maturer genius delighted to present those whose
power is in intellect and noble qualities of heart,
the virtues that endure.

He views woman primarily from the standpoint of sex. The woman conquers, where she
conquers at all, not because of her knowledge,
not because of her keener intuitions or her developed power to struggle and attain, but because of her sex-relations. Her jealousies
sharpen her wits, the charms of her woman's nature bring warriors to her feet, and by her loves

[1] P. 6.

she makes and unmakes men and kingdoms.
Vivian conquers Merlin. Guinevere dooms the
round table to dissolution. The Princess as a
college president is a feminine fizzle, but as the
beloved of the amorous prince she is winsome,
strong, and womanly. She finds her true self
and her place in the world by loyalty to sex-in-
stincts and by the performance of sex-functions.
Margaret is besought not to enter the toil of life.[2]
At every crossroads the poet erected a guide-
post pointing lonely maidens to the

> larger woman-world
> Of wives and mothers.[3]

This is not, to the poet's mind, belittling
woman's nature, or her work in the world. It is
only saying that her nature is not the same as
man's, and that her mission in the world is determined by her natural capacities, tastes, and
endowments. He really holds up to condemnation a false idea of woman by putting into the
mouth of the upstart, raving youth of Locksley
Hall such words as these:

> Woman's pleasure, woman's pain —
> Nature made them blinder motions bounded in a shal-
>   lower brain:

[2] P. 21.
[3] "The Ring," p. 821.

Woman is the lesser man, and all thy passions, matched
    with mine,
Are as moonlight unto sunlight, and as water unto
    wine.[4]

He does not sanction the theories of Lady Psyche
and Lady Blanche, who maintained

             that with equal husbandry
    The woman were an equal to the man.

He does not join in the effort of the Princess,

    To lift the woman's fallen divinity
    Upon an even pedestal with man.[5]

Much less does he approve of the low ideal of the
fat-faced curate, Edward Bull:

    God made the woman for the use of man,
    And for the good and increase of the world.[6]

On the contrary, he demands that we

        let this proud watchword rest of Equal . . . .
    For woman is not undevelopt man
    But diverse.[7]

If it be true, as one lecturer in the Princess' college affirmed, that woman's progress has been retarded by prejudice and custom and convention,
these fetters should be broken. The right to

[4] P. 102.
[5] P. 183.
[6] "Edwin Morris," p. 84.
[7] "The Princess," p. 214.

freedom is the inalienable right of every soul.
But the fundamental fact is this that

> either sex alone
> Is half itself, and in true marriage lies
> Nor equal, nor unequal: each fulfils
> Defect in each, and always thought in thought,
> Purpose in purpose, will in will, they grow,
> The single, pure and perfect animal,
> The two-celled heart beating, with one full stroke,
> Life.[8]

This summarizes the poet's doctrine of the significance of sex-differences and of woman's proper partnership with man, especially in the family.

Tennyson also puts strong and repeated emphasis upon the motherhood function of woman. With this is often connected her peculiar gift of ministry as nurse in hospital or home. It was Psyche,

> The mother of the sweetest little maid,
> That ever crow'd for kisses,

to whom Florian addressed the question,

> are you
> That, Psyche, wont to bind my throbbing brow,
> To smooth my pillow, mix the foaming draught
> Of fever, tell me pleasant tales, and read
> My sickness down to happy dreams?[9]

[8] *Loc. cit.*
[9] *Ibid.,* p. 177.

The influence of the child of Psyche upon the Princess and her colleagues is evidence of the truth of the statement that

> The bearing and the training of a child
> Is woman's wisdom.[10]

Perhaps Tennyson's own mother had by her character and life impressed this doctrine most deeply upon him, for it was she who is portrayed as his ideal in the beautiful passage:

> One
> Not learned, save in gracious household ways,
> Not perfect, nay, but full of tender wants,
> No Angel, but a dearer being, all dipt
> In Angel instincts, breathing Paradise,
> Interpreter between the Gods and men,
> Who look'd all native to her place, and yet
> On tiptoe seem'd to touch upon a sphere
> Too gross to tread, and all male minds perforce
> Sway'd to her from their orbits as they moved,
> And girdled her with music. Happy he
> With such a mother! Faith in woman kind
> Beats with his blood, and trust in all things high
> Comes easy to him, and tho' he trip and fall
> He shall not blind his soul with clay.[11]

How much this means to all our world is hinted by Becket, who finds a wild-fowl frozen upon a nest of ice-cold eggs, and exclaims:

[10] *Ibid.*, p. 202.
[11] *Ibid.*, p. 215.

Look! how this love, this mother, runs thro' all
The world God made — even the beast — the bird! [12]

This is one of the mighty forces in our world, and it is a permanent force. Demeter in Enna feels within herself " the deathless heart of motherhood." [13] Robin in the forest shows how great was the influence of his mother upon him. For her sake " and the blessed Queen of Heaven " he reverences all women. Tennyson's mother being to him the revelation of God, it is not strange that he ever showed to her that consideration and love which could not escape the notice of his friends.[14] In a letter to his aunt he speaks of her as " one of the most angelick natures on God's earth, always doing good as it were by a sort of intuition." She who in later years became the mother of his children revealed to him still more of the divinity of motherhood and exalted in his mind this function of woman in the progress of the race.[15]

The secret of the mother's power in the world is not a mystery. Tennyson's philosophy is here at one with all his philosophy of life. The mightiest forces in the universe are spiritual, and of all the spiritual forces the most powerful is

[12] " Becket," Act V, sc. 2, p. 742.
[13] " Demeter and Persephone," p. 807.
[14] *Memoir*, Vol. I, p. 77.
[15] *Ibid.*, p. 331.

love.   In Tennyson's boyhood home the mother
" ruled by right of love."   This was a lesson
which the poet never forgot.   From it he learned
that " love is the greatest thing in the world."

As far back as 1847 the poet's friends quote
him as saying that one of the two great social
questions impending in England was " the higher
education of women." [16]   This remarkable insight into the social problems of the future is
shown again and again in the poems.   " The
Princess " is in reality a treatise upon the higher
education of women.   It holds up to ridicule the
theory that the woman is only undeveloped man,
and needs the same education as he in order to
attain her best.   He is sure that " the sooner
woman finds out, before the great educational
movement begins, that woman is not undeveloped
man, but diverse," the better it will be for the
progress of the world.[17]   The Princess is a plea
for such training for woman as shall best fit
her to perform her own work in the world.
This is not the same as that of man, but is
peculiar to herself.   In the tragedy of " Queen
Mary " Bagenhall speaks of Lady Jane as one
whose attainments are those of the ideal young
woman.

[16] *Ibid.*, p. 249.
[17] *Ibid.*, p. 249.

Seventeen — and knew eight languages; in music
Peerless — her needle perfect, and her learning
Beyond the churchmen; yet so meek, so modest,
So wife-like humble to the trivial boy
Mismatch'd with her for policy![18]

The actual woman of the time is more accurately
sketched in a nonsense speech of Dora in " The
Promise of May." She says: " Can't I speak
like a lady; pen a letter like a lady; talk a little
French like a lady; play a little like a lady?"[19]

Remembering the time that " The Princess"
was published (1847), we may well call it the
" herald-melody" of the higher education of
women. Tennyson himself considered the princess Ida as one of the noblest of his feminine creations. The higher in her subdued the lower.
In the end she was true to her obligation to the
social order and to God.

He disliked pedantry in women, and never hesi-
tated to say so. Hallam Tennyson thus sums up
his father's teaching upon this subject:

She (woman) must train herself to do the large
work that lies before her, even though she may not be
destined to be wife or mother, cultivating her understanding not her memory only, her imagination in its
highest phases, her inborn spirituality and her sympathy with all that is pure, noble and beautiful, rather

[18] Act III, sc. 1, p. 608.
[19] Act III, p. 798.

than mere social accomplishments; then, and then only, will she further the progress of humanity, then, and then only, men will continue to hold her in reverence.[20]

[20] *Memoir,* Vol. I, p. 250.

CHAPTER V

THE FAMILY

The essential freedom of the soul was one of the fundamental postulates of all Tennyson's thinking. He would admit the divine right of no convention, law, or ruler to annihilate that freedom. His problem, then, was to construct an ideal social state, with all its necessary laws and institutions, which would also give to the individual the liberty to which he has an inalienable right. The primary social body whose existence makes possible the larger combinations of society is the family. Here, then, the problem was first confronted. How shall the family be organized and maintained so that every member shall possess that peculiar freedom which is his right, while at the same time the family is made to perform its proper function in the social organism?

The volume of 1830 contained " The Poet." This poem has one stanza which refers primarily to the French Revolution, but which has also a certain application to the formal rite by which the family is established:

> And Freedom rear'd in that august sunrise
>   Her beautiful bold brow,
> When rites and forms before his burning eyes
>   Melted like snow.[1]

If marriage is a form or rite which stands as a
barrier to the onward march of Freedom, then
it must be torn away. But all freedom, political
and personal, is gained not by ignorance or scorn
of righteous law, but by obedience to it. Edgar
in " The Promise of May " argues that the man,
by flinging aside " the morals of his tribe and
following his own instincts as his God,

> Will enter on the larger golden age.[2]

His objection to the *bond* of marriage is stated
thus:

> If you *will* bind love to one forever,
> Altho' at first he takes his bonds for flowers,
> As years go on, he feels them press upon him,
> Begins to flutter in them, and at last
> Breaks thro' them, and so flies away for ever;
> While had you left him free use of his wings,
> Who knows that he had ever dreamed of flying?[2]

Such words in the mouth of such a man as Edgar
commend that which they seem to condemn.
Edgar's condemnation of marriage is really an
argument for the social necessity of the marriage
bond. Edgar was himself a failure, and the

[1] P. 14.
[2] Act I, pp. 784, 785.

practical consequences of living his theories brand his creed as failure.   Marriage, then, is one of the essentials for the stability of the family and the progress of society.   " The Wreck " [3] has the necessity of marriage as its moral, though at the same time it demonstrates that no law is so just as not at times to be unjust to an occasional individual.   If injustice ever be done, it must be endured for the sake of the larger good to society.   Yet even to the individual, marriage is necessary for the completed life of either man or woman.   This is the conclusion of the experiment of " The Princess." [4]

There is, however, a very strong insistence upon the higher motive for marriage.   It is not difficult to detect in such lines as these in " Edwin Morris," the real contempt felt by the poet for the wedding when Mammon is the priest:

> She went, and in one month
> They wedded her to sixty thousand pounds,
> To lands in Kent, and messuages in York,
> And slight Sir Robert with his watery smile
> And educated whisker.[5]

The crime and sorrow of such an alliance are shown again and again.   The woman betrothed

[3] P. 541.
[4] *Memoir,* Vol. I, p. 249.
[5] P. 85.

to one whose face she loathes to see, in order to
save the ancestral estate, calls to her sister:

Come, speak a little comfort! all night I pray'd with
    tears,
And yet no comfort came to me, and now the morn
    appears,
When he will tear me from your side, who bought me
    for his slave;
This father pays his debt with me, and weds me to my
    grave.[6]

Dora, in " The Promise of May " is confronted
by a similar condition, and is tempted to marry
Farmer Dobson, whom she " can't abide," because in the financial straits of her family he
could " keep their heads above water." [7]   He is,
when matched with her Harold, " like a hedge
thistle by a garden rose."   Harold was not the
" garden rose " she had imagined him, but this
mistake did not make marriage for money more
worthy of approval in her eyes.

So likewise in " The Foresters " Marian was
urged by old Sir Richard to marry one who
would pay the mortgage, and the maid spurned
the suggestion with all the strength of her resolute soul.   Money and land were to her as nothing compared with her love for Robin.[8]   There

[6] " The Flight," p. 552.
[7] P. 796.
[8] P. 840.

are many other places in the poems where Tennyson's contempt for such a motive for marriage
is clearly shown.   Mr. Aubrey de Vere tells of
a rebuke administered by the poet to a young
lady who sat next to him one day at dinner and
spoke of a certain marriage just announced as a
very penniless one.   He rummaged in his pocket,
pulled out a penny and slapped it down loudly
close to her plate, saying: "There, I give you
that, for that is the God you worship!" [9]   The
frequency with which money appears in the
poems as the motive for marriage is an indication of the power of this motive in the formation
of matrimonial alliances in Tennyson's day.   To
give to it a truthful representation in verse was
in itself a social service, for thus he held the
mirror to his time.   The vision of the reality
was the condemnation of that which was seen.
Tennyson's scorn of the thing condemned is in
his representation of it.

Marriage is too sacred to be the slave of policy,
the poet believes.   To be sure, the dying Edward
in the drama of "Harold" exclaims:

> and a wife,
> What matter who, so she be serviceable
> In all obedience, as mine own hath been: [10]

[9] *Memoir*, Vol. I, p. 289.
[10] Act III, sc. 1, p. 673.

but it was a weak man who gave expression to
that low sentiment.   Even Edith urges Harold
to marry Lady Aldwyth:

> If this be politic,
> And well for thee and England — and for her —
> Care not for me who love thee.[11]

Such doctrine was not novel to Aldwyth, who
declares to Harold that her former marriage to
the king of Wales was " a match of policy.[12]   By
this experience she had, as it were, got her hand
in, and so was ready for another match of policy.
The unfortunate result of such a marriage is
given by Harold:

> I married her for Morcar — a sin against
> The truth of love.   Evil for good, it seems,
> Is oft as childless of the good as evil
> For evil.[13]

Mary's plea for her marriage to Philip was a plea
for policy.   She says:

> If it might please God that I should leave
> Some fruit of mine own body after me,
> To be your king, ye would rejoice thereat,
> And it would be your comfort, as I trust.
>
> .   .   .   .
>
> Moreover, if this marriage should not seem,
> Before our own High Court of Parliament,

[11] Act III, sc. 1, p. 676.
[12] Act IV, sc. 1, p. 679.
[13] Act V, sc. 1, p. 685.

> To be of rich advantage to our realm,
> We will refrain, and not alone from this,
> Likewise from any other.[14]

Sternly rejecting all such motives as these for entering upon the marriage relation, Tennyson taught that marriage is of the soul, not of the body.[15] Marian, the heroine of " The Foresters," refuses to wed the sheriff for gold or the prince for policy, but clings to the outcast Robin whom she loves. A marriage thus motived lends reason to the belief of the poor that " marriages are made in Heaven." [16] It is only a man of the spirit of the Northern Farmer, whose greed has become blood in his horse's legs that say " proputty, proputty, proputty," who could give to a son such instruction as this:

> Thou'll not marry for munny — thou's sweet upo'
>   parson's lass —
> Noa — thou'll marry for luvv — an' we boath on us
>   thinks tha an ass.[17]

Eleanor, in the tragedy of " Becket," speaks lightly of the affection of husband for wife and of wife for husband; but the heroic Becket reproves her: " Madam, you do ill to scorn wedded love." [18] How sincere and pure and

[14] " Queen Mary," Act II, sc. 2, p. 599.

[15] " The Foresters," Act IV, sc. 1, p. 868.

[16] " Aylmer's Field," p. 145.

[17] *Poems,* p. 231.

[18] " Prologue," p. 697.

deep that love is which binds two souls together
in ennobling wedlock is more clearly shown by
the results of such a marriage than by lowering
any psychological plummet into the depth of love
itself. Before the true marriage can be con-
summated, God must have wrought " two spirits
to one equal mind." [19] When that has been
wrought, the husband, understanding the sacredness and full significance of the relationship upon
which he has entered, can say to his chosen:

> In the name of wife,
>   And in the rights that name may give,
> Are clasped the moral of thy life,
>   And that for which I care to live.[20]

This does not mean the subjection of one to the
other. There is here no slavery, but the completed life for each. The lover declares to the
Princess:

> my hopes and thine are one:
> Accomplish thou my manhood and thyself.[21]

Even to the Lotos-Eaters, the memory of wedded
life was dear.[22] Love increased in purity and
strength with the years. In later life the husband thought of the one whom he had known

---

[19] " The Miller's Daughter," p. 39.
[20] " The Day Dream L'Envoi," p. 108.
[21] *Poems*, p. 215.
[22] *Ibid.*, p. 55.

most intimately in the sacred relation of the family as

> the idol of my youth,
> The darling of my manhood, and alas!
> Now the most blessed memory of mine age.[23]

Though this poem was written before Tennyson's own marriage, these words are a true statement of his own growing affection for his wife. " The peace of God came into my life before the altar when I wedded her," he declared in afterdays.[24]   The obligation of husband to wife and of wife to husband is the obligation imposed by the purest love.   Each should seek the most complete and perfect development of the noblest powers of the other.   The relation is not that of master and servant, but of two godlike souls indissolubly bound together, not as equals, but " like in difference," growing liker in the long years," each fulfilling defect in each until they become " the two-celled heart beating, with one full stroke, Life." [25]

The proverbial perversity of Cupid, and the dramatic possibilities of the treatment of love between those of different rank, naturally suggest the frequent recurrence of this situation in the poems.   Tennyson's use of this situation is, how-

[23] " Gardener's Daughter," p. 77.
[24] *Memoir*, Vol. I, p. 329.
[25] " Princess," p. 214.

ever, traditional rather than original. There is variety in his dramatic representation of the problem, and in his portrayal of the actors in the drama, but his solution of the difficulty, if indeed it can be called a solution at all, is neither new nor striking. He gives noble emphasis to the truth that it is character and not rank that makes the man or the woman. In " Lady Clara Vere de Vere " there is perhaps the strongest and most beautiful statement of this principle as related to the possibility of marriage between those of different rank. It was much for an Englishman to say

> A simple maiden in her flower
> Is worth a hundred coat-of-arms.
>
> . . . .
>
> Trust me, Clara Vere de Vere,
>   From yon blue heavens above us bent
> The gardener Adam and his wife
>   Smile at the claims of long descent.
> Howe'er it be, it seems to me,
>   'Tis only noble to be good.
> Kind hearts are more than coronets,
>   And simple faith than Norman blood.[26]

Despite this fine statement, when " the daughter of a cottager " wedded Sir Edward Head, she was declared to be " out of her sphere," and only unhappiness was the result.[27] When the Lord

[26] " Lady Clara Vere de Vere," p. 49.
[27] " Walking to the Mail," p. 82.

of Burleigh loved and wed a village maiden, he
unknowingly brought upon her " the burthen of
an honour unto which she was not born," and

So she droop'd and droop'd before him.

. . . .

Then before her time she died.[28]

In " In Memoriam " the poet compares

some poor girl whose heart is set
On one whose rank exceeds her own,[29]

to himself as he thinks longingly of Hallam in
his higher life beyond the grave.   Such a com-
parison inevitably suggests to the reader that in
the mind of Tennyson between those of different
rank there was a great gulf fixed.   For man or
woman to pass that gulf and join hands with one
loved on the further side in happy marriage was
indeed difficult.

This is the poet's recognition of a fact, an
actual condition in the society of his time.   This
does not imply that he approved of that which he
portrayed.   There is reason to believe that he
distinctly disapproved of it.   Lady Clare stills
weds Lord Ronald and presumably " lives happy
ever after," even when it is known that she is
only the daughter of the nurse and not Lady
Clare at all.[30]   King Cophetua likewise

[28] " The Lord of Burleigh," p. 117.
[29] LX, p. 262.
[30] " Lady Clare," p. 114.

sware a royal oath:
This beggar maid shall be my queen![31]

Such lines as " Ring out false pride in place and
blood " [32] indicate that into these poems he puts
his own thought and conviction.   He knew that
" The thrall in person may be free in soul." [33]
He had and expressed a contempt for the " snob-
bery of English society," [34] whatever form it
took.   In what was originally verse III in
" Maud " he thus holds up to derision the " Lord-
Captain up at the Hall " :

> Captain ! he to hold command !
> He can hold a cue, he can pocket a ball ;
> And sure not a bantam cockerel lives
> With a weaker crow upon English land,
> Whether he boast of a horse that gains,
> Or cackle his own applause.[35]

Such portrayals of rank without character reveal
unmistakably Tennyson's own thought of the
true relation of members of one class to those of
another.   His appeal was to reality, not to name
or place.   Where souls were joined together in
enduring love he knew that no false pride of rank

[31] " The Beggar Maid," p. 119.
[32] " In Memoriam," CVI., p. 278.
[33] " Gareth and Lynette," p. 320.
[34] *Memoir*, Vol. I, p. 278.
[35] *Ibid.*, p. 403.

should put them asunder.   Yet that marriage between those of different social station often
meant keen suffering for sensitive souls of the
lower class who became partners in such an alliance, he frankly avowed.

He was himself an ardent lover of children and
a firm believer in the exalted mission of children
in the family and the state.   He has little sympathy with the parent who tyrannizes over the
child and makes his own word or whim a law
which the child must blindly obey.   The father
in the poem of " Dora " is such an unpitying
tyrant.[36]   The child who has come to years of
discretion and still remains the " puppet to a
father's threat " [37] is deserving of little respect.
Parental love that is intelligent and strong will
demand and receive an obedience that is ready
and glad.   Children bind parents together in a
holier love and exalt the family as the defense
of society.   It was a child that called forth the
tender affection of Guinevere, and caused her for
a moment to forget herself and her cares till the
little Nestling past from her.[38]   Later it was a
child within the nunnery walls who became the
companion of the despairing queen, and while in-
nocently wounding her with tales of the wicked

[36] P. 77.
[37] " Locksley Hall," p. 99.
[38] " The Last Tournament," p. 443.

consort of the noble Arthur, yet at the same time aroused in her the high ambitions which aided in her redemption. One cannot help wondering what influence the Nestling would have had upon the character of the queen if the babe had lived. Would Guinevere and the Round Table have thus been saved? The child is really the heroine of " The Princess " and brings the college to sanity and success.

The importance of the child to the family and to society gives to the perils that threaten him very great significance. One of the children of Enoch Arden died because of poverty, or because the mother's business often called her from home. This was but one of many such innocent sufferers. In " Maud " we read of the time

When a Mammonite mother kills her babe for a burial
   fee,
And Timour-mammon grins on a pile of children's
   bones.[39]

Farther on in the same poem he declares that all the arsenic is used up in poisoning the babes.[40] The spinster in the dialect poem " The Spinster's Sweet-Arts " says: " I niver not wish'd fur childer, I hevn't naw likin' fur brats; " [41] and she is recognized as the representative of a class.

[39] P. 287.
[40] P. 306.
[41] P. 559.

Thousands of unwelcome children are born on crowded streets, and "city children soak and blacken soul and sense in city slime." [42]   These are facts to be reckoned with by the poet, who is also a student of society, who knows of the significance of the child to the family and to the state.   He condemned the Cambridge of 1830 because it stood apart from its age,

> Because the lips of little children preach
> Against you, you that do profess to teach
> And teach us nothing, feeding not the heart. [43]

A favorite saying of his was: "Make the lives of children as beautiful and as happy as possible." [44]   The perils of society caused by the neglect or abuse of children he would seek to banish by making the life of every child bright and joyous.

That the poet was not without interest and belief in the doctrine of heredity is evidenced by various passages in the poems. Speaking of " Maud " he says:

> Some peculiar, mystic grace
> Made her only the child of her mother,
> And heap'd the whole inherited sin
> On that huge scapegoat of the race,
> All, all upon the brother. [45]

[42] "Locksley Hall Sixty Years After," p. 566.
[43] *Memoir,* Vol. I, p. 67.
[44] *Ibid.,* p. 371.
[45] Sec. 13, p. 295.

Balin looked with profound admiration upon
Lancelot and marveled that he himself was so far
surpassed by this favorite of the king, muttering:

> These be gifts,
> Born with the blood, not learnable, divine,
> Beyond *my reach*.[46]

The wife and mother who had deserted her husband and child for a man who was a dwarf in
stature but a giant in intellect, when she made
her confession to her mother, sought to comfort
herself with the words: " But if sin be sin, not
inherited fate, as many will say." [47] The *Ancient Sage* takes up the theme and says:

> In the fatal sequence of this world
> An evil thought may soil thy children's blood.[48]

" Locksley Hall Sixty Years After " gives us a
cautious yet positive statement of the same doctrine:

> She the worldling born of worldlings — father, mother
> — be content,
> Ev'n the homely farm can teach us there is something
> in descent.[49]

But the most dramatic portrayal of the principle
occurs in " The Promise of May," in which the
poet puts into the mouth of Harold the words:

[46] " Balin and Balan," p. 372.
[47] " The Wreck," p. 543.
[48] *Poems,* pp. 551, 552.
[49] P. 561.

> O this mortal house,
> Which we are born into, is haunted by
> The ghosts of the dead passions of dead men;
> And these take flesh again with our own flesh,
> And bring us to confusion.[50]

His belief in heredity was to him, however, not a cause for despair, but rather a call to conflict. In the course of his talk with a young man who was going to the university he said: "The real test of a man is not what he knows, but what he is in himself and in his relation to others. For instance, can he battle against his own bad inherited instincts, or brave public opinion in the cause of truth." [51]   Tennyson not only believed and taught that bad inherited instincts may be conquered, but himself sounded the call to battle with those instincts.

Perhaps no writer has ever given to the world pictures of English home and country life more original and beautiful in form than those given by Tennyson in such poems as "The Gardener's Daughter," "Dora," "Audley Court," "The Talking Oak," "Locksley Hall," "Godiva," "Lady Clare," "The Lord of Burleigh," and several others. He believed and taught that the stability and greatness of a nation depend largely upon the home life of the people. He had true

[50] Act II, p. 789.
[51] Memoir, Vol. I, p. 318.

joy in the family duties and affections. It is only the simple truth to say, as his son has said, that this was one of the secrets of his power over mankind.[52]

[52] *Ibid.,* p. 189.

CHAPTER VI

SOCIETY

It is not to be expected that a poet, viewing life from the standpoint of the artist, will deal largely in the technical terms of the sociologist. A man may have an important message to deliver concerning the needs and destiny of society, even though he use some other phrase than "the social organism" to embody his profoundest thought. We shall look in vain in the writings of Tennyson for terms which are regarded by some as words of magic in social science. He has none such. Practical students of sociology will regard this as a virtue rather than a defect. What he has to say of the nature and vices and mission of human society he says as a poet. He is, to be sure, especially attracted by the dramatic phases of the social problem, but these are to him, after all, only outward signs of inner conditions, only incidents in a journey whose end no man can clearly foresee nor fully foretell. His critics accused him of living in the past. Carlyle described him to Sir J. Simeon as " sitting on a dung-heap among innumerable dead dogs." [1]

[1] *Memoir*, Vol. I, p. 340.

He said of himself: "The far future has been my world always." [2] He did study the past and sing of its greatest achievements, but the past was to him a prophecy of the future. He did live in the far future as his world, but it is a future which is the natural fulfilment of the prophecies of the present and the past.

His ideal of society is really determined by his ideal of man. Man is a free spiritual being dwelling in a body. He is in part a product of evolution, yet aspires after infinitely greater things than he has ever attained. Endowed with such unmeasured capacities crying for development, he has claims for recognition in the social body which must not be ignored. In general, the interests of the individual and the interests of society are one, but there are times when this seems not to be the fact. The well-being of society is largely dependent upon the sacredness of the family. The highest interests of the family are largely dependent upon the sanctity of the marriage bond. That sanctity must be maintained, even though it seems to work hardship for the individual. This is well illustrated in "The Wreck."

The exception gives added weight to the rule. He entitles his lines on pantheism "The Higher Pantheism," because, unlike this doctrine in the

[2] *Ibid.*, p. 168.

East, he gives the individual full and free action. This poem recognizes the universal without obscuring the individual. The " Flower in the Crannied Wall " expresses essentially the same thought. Science has by its vast conceptions tended to give man a relatively lower place in the great cosmic world. The poet calls us back to the true idea of the individual, and shows the real relation which exists between the progress of man and that of society. As man advances, society progresses. The exception just cited is more apparent than real, for Tennyson makes large use of the doctrine of self-sacrifice. It is only as the individual loses his own life for the sake of love that he saves it for himself and for society. There is then no actual inconsistency between the lines in " Amphion,"

> And I must work thro' months of toil,
>   And years of cultivation,
> Upon my proper patch of soil
>   To grow my own plantation.[3]

and the more exalted spirit of the " Ode on the Death of the Duke of Wellington,"

> Who cares not to be great
> But as he saves or serves the state.[4]

There is here no chance for asceticism. Every true man says of himself: " I will not shut me

[3] P. 109.
[4] P. 220.

from my kind." [5] He comes so near to his fellow-men of different creed and color that he can
" cull from every faith and race the best," [6] and
at the same time give to others the best he has
gained from his own life-experience. This is
really the best preparation that anyone can have
to answer the questions which the poet imagines
the Almighty to ask everyone who appears before
him in the next life: " Have you been true to
yourself and given in My Name a cup of cold
water to one of these little ones? " [7] He does
not cry out against the age as hopelessly bad, but
tries to show wherein it is wrong, in order that
each individual may do his best to redeem it.
The evils he denounces are individual, and can
be cured only as each man looks to his own
heart.[8] This has real meaning for society, for he
held that each individual has a spiritual and eternal significance with relation to other individual
wills.[9]

Tennyson came to the noble conception of
human society as a great brotherhood, but he arrived at that destination via his own England.
It seems hardly thinkable now that he could have

[5] " In Memoriam," CVIII. p. 278.
[6] " Akbar's Dream," p. 879.
[7] *Memoir*, Vol. I, p. 309.
[8] *Ibid.*, p. 468.
[9] *Ibid.*, p. 319

been so chilled by the cold reception given his earlier poems as seriously to consider changing his residence to Jersey or the south of France or Italy.[10]   One could scarcely think of Tennyson as living anywhere except in England.   He was English to the core.   He said:

> That man's the best Cosmopolite
> Who loves his native country best,[11]

and there could be no better illustration of the statement than Tennyson himself.   His patriotic stanzas give ample evidence that it was his own conviction that

> there's no glory
> Like his who saves his country.[12]

It was not, however, a narrow, insular England to which he gave his heart's devotion, but the England of broad domain, of many peoples, and with a noble destiny to fulfil as the divine benefactor of the world.   It was to him " the eye, the soul of Europe," and he called upon statesmen to

> Keep our noble England whole,
> And save the one true seed of freedom sown
> Betwixt a people and their ancient throne,
> That sober freedom out of which there springs
> Our loyal passion for our temperate kings;

[10] *Memoir,* Vol. I, p. 97.
[11] " Hands All Round," p. 575.
[12] " Queen Mary," p. 595.

For, saving that, ye help to save mankind
Till public wrong be crumbled into dust,
And drill the raw world for the march of mind,
Till crowds at length be sane, and crowns be just.[13]

He further declares in " The Third of February : "

No little German state are we
But the one voice in Europe.[14]

This judgment of the position of England among
the powers of the world was justified by history.
It was not a new thing for this great land to con-
tend for liberty. We have " fought for freedom
from our prime," he cried.[15]   With such a past
the Foresters could sing with all the enthusiasm
of their sturdy natures:

There is no land like England
Where'er the light of day be;
There are no hearts like English hearts
Such hearts of oak as they be.[16]

When he cried, " Britons, guard your own," he
called upon his people to defend that which had
the deepest significance for the world as well as
for themselves.   To be true to their own past was
to be true to their highest and widest world-
destiny.[17]   England was to him " the little isle

[13] " Ode on the Death of the Duke of Wellington," p. 220.
[14] P. 221.
[15] P. 222.
[16] " The Foresters," Act II, sc. 1, p. 846.
[17] *Memoir*, Vol. I, p. 344.

where a man may still be true," [18] and everywhere the one who is true to himself cannot be
false to any man. In one of the closing lines of
" Maud " we have a statement of a conclusion
arrived at after much struggle, and which shows
the natural progress from love of country to
union with all mankind: " I have felt with my
native land, I am one with my kind." [19] This
conclusion is reached despite a frank admission
of Britain's gravest faults, her " lust for gold,"
her adoration of " her one sole God — the mil-
lionaire," [20] and all the vices usually attendant
upon such lust and gross idolatry.

Such individual and social crimes are not peculiar to the people of his England. They are
everywhere. As they are traitors to the reign
of love in one land, so they war against the forces
of human brotherhood everywhere, seeking to
advance and take possession of the world. Now

we cannot be kind to each other here for an hour!
We whisper and hint and chuckle, and grin at a
brother's shame,[21]

whether that brother be in our own or in another
land. It is not a great extension of the patriotic
conception to include in the national brotherhood

[18] *Loc. cit.,* p. 438.
[19] P. 308.
[20] P. 307.
[21] " Maud," p. 290.

the " Indian brothers " who fought bravely in
" The Defence of Lucknow." [22]   A common flag
does much to assure those who fight under it
that they are one people.   It is much more significant when he says, in his lines " To Victor
Hugo " :

> England, France, all man to be
> Will make one people ere man's race be run.[23]

France was the land of revolution where was the
" red, fool fury of the Seine; " and everyone
knows how cordially Tennyson hated these bloody
outbreaks of the lawless spirit.

To include the people of France in his thought
of the coming brotherhood was a distinct advance.   Still further progress in the same direction is chronicled in the " Epilogue," where these
words occur:

> Slav, Teuton, Kelt, I count them all
> My friends and brother souls,
> With all the peoples, great and small,
> That wheel between the poles.[24]

We do not wonder that such a citizen of the
world and lover of mankind sees in vision " all
the millions one at length." [25]   Where there is
a oneness of the millions, where one individual

[22] P. 520.
[23] P. 534.
[24] P. 570.
[25] " Locksley Hall Sixty Years After," p. 564.

will has a definite spiritual significance to other individual wills, love and mutual service are to be confidently expected. When the practical motto is "all for each and each for all," [26] it will not be long to wait

> Till each man find his own in all men's good,
> And all men work in noble brotherhood. [27]

This is the complete and perfected society of which Tennyson dreamed, universal in its scope, unselfish in its motive, noble and pure in the love which binds all together in mutual service.

But this condition has not yet been attained. Society is not yet a brotherhood. It is divided into classes which are mutually antagonistic. There are oppression and greed on the one hand, and rebellion and hatred and open conflict on the other. There are tyranny and crime and war in the world. How to change the actual conditions of human society today into the ideal state which the poet has conceived, is the problem. In the "Miller's Daughter" there is an indication of the existence of a social problem. In "Lady Clare" there is a more definite statement of the great question:

[26] *Loc. cit.,* p. 564.
[27] "Ode at International Exhibition," p. 223.

These two parties still divide the world —
Of those that want, and those that have; and still
The same old sore breaks out from age to age.[28]

The English lord is frequently portrayed as
wholly unworthy of rank or honor. The city
clerk, whose gains were small and whose work
was hard, was a representative of a large and unfortunate class.[29] " The sons of the glebe scowled
at their great lord." [30] They knew his life as
servants know the lives of their masters. But
the rich know little or nothing of the lives of the
poor. Robin Hood, an outlaw, was declared by
Sir Richard to be the truest friend of the people,[31] and Robin himself said that the " gentler "
know naught " o' the food o' the poor." [32] In
" Locksley Hall Sixty Years After " these sensible words are spoken to the young Leonard:

You, my Leonard, use and not abuse your day,
Move among your people, know them, follow him who
led the way,
Strove for sixty widow'd years to help his homlier
brother men,
Served the poor, and built the cottage, raised the
school, and drain'd the fen.[33]

[28] " Walking to the Mail," p. 82.
[29] " Sea Dreams," p. 156.
[30] " Aylmer's Field," p. 153.
[31] " The Foresters," Act I, sc. 1, p. 840.
[32] *Ibid.,* Act II, sc. 1, p. 849.
[33] P. 567.

The poet was in his own life true to this teaching of his verse. His son informs us that the severest punishment he ever received from his father was for some want of respect to one of their servants.[34]

Tennyson does not fail to recognize the presence of noble qualities in those of high rank, as in the man who left his wine and horses and play to sit with Maud in her sickness, to read to her night and day and tend her like a nurse.[35] But the reader is never left with the impression that such nobleness of character is the result of rank. Tennyson puts his own conviction into such words as those uttered by Sir Gareth to the maiden declaring that the knave that does service as full knight is all as good as any knight.[36] " The gentler born the more bound to be serviceable." [37] In " Queen Mary " the Lords are bought with Philip's gold.[38] Becket speaks of the

> baron-brutes
> That havock'd all the land in Stephen's day.[39]

Dobson, in " The Promise of May," solves the whole problem at a stroke and cries: " Damn

---

[34] *Memoir,* Vol. I, p. 370.
[35] " Maud," p. 299.
[36] " Gareth and Lynette," p. 334.
[37] " Lancelot and Elaine," p. 408.
[38] Act III, sc. I, p. 605.
[39] " Becket," Act I, sc. I, p. 701.

all gentlemen, says I." [40]   Robin, in " The Foresters," speaks of " these proud priests, and these
Barons, Devils, that make this blessed England
hell." [41]   Friar Tuck threatens Prince John and
mutters of him to the sheriff: " He may be
prince; he is not gentleman." [42]   In a letter to
Mrs. Russell, written in 1847, the poet puts into
prose something of his feeling toward those of
rank. He says: " Why do all English country
gentlemen talk of dogs, horses, roads, crops, etc?
It is better after all than affecting Art and Feeling: they would make a poor hand of that, though
you tried to help them out. I wish they would
be a little kinder to the poor. I would honor
them then and they might talk what they
would." [43]

Wealth and rank are at least supposed to go
together. There are so many exceptions to this
statement that practical people are often inclined
to construe it as a " supposition contrary to fact."
Wealth is, however, a co-worker with rank in dividing society into classes and postponing the
dawn of the day of universal brotherhood. The
possession of wealth imposes the obligation to
serve, but many who possess it are not kind to

[40] Act II, p. 793.
[41] Act III, sc. 1, p. 857.
[42] *Ibid.*, Act IV, sc. 1, p. 807.
[43] *Memoir,* Vol. I, p. 243.

the poor. When they bestow help upon those who are in need, they throw their gifts carelessly as those " who care not how they give." [44] " The gold that gilds the straiten'd forehead of the fool " [45] is only a curse to the one who possesses it and to the society in which he moves. It is only wealth wisely used that is a blessing to the world. The love of money for its own sake leads to corruption in society and the separation of man from his brother. " Every door is barr'd with gold, and opens but to golden keys," and " the jingling of the guinea helps the hurt that Honour feels.[46]

But there are other truthful accusations to be laid at the door of humanity-corrupting gold:

> This filthy marriage-hindering Mammon made
> The harlot of the cities."[47]

" Cowardice " is " the child of lust for gold." [48] The Earl of Devon was an example of a class and of him Mary speaks as

> the fool —
> He wrecks his health and wealth on courtesans,
> And rolls himself in carrion like a dog."[49]

[44] " Tithonus," p. 96.
[45] " Locksley Hall," p. 99.
[46] *Ibid.,* p. 100.
[47] " Aylmer's Field," p. 148.
[48] " To the Queen," p. 475.
[49] " Queen Mary," Act I, sc. 5, p. 58.

The press of a thousand cities has felt the influence of this corrupting power, and "easily vio-
lates virgin Truth for a coin or a cheque." [50]
Against the worship of this money-god the poet
gave his voice and his example. In time of
threatened financial loss which would mean much
to him, his wife wrote: "A. showed a noble
disregard of money, much as the loss would af-
fect us." [51] The first canto of "Maud" Tennyson was accustomed to read aloud in a sort of
rushing recitative through the long sweeping
lines of satire and invective against the greed for
money.[52] He was often in need of money himself, but he never could or would write a line for
it. That would have been to him the perversion
of his art.[53]

He looked forward to the coming of a nobler
spirit into society — a spirit that masters wealth
and insists upon making it, not the destruction
of the few through luxury and excess, but the
servant of the many through intelligent, unselfish
use for the good of the world. So he calls:
"Ring out the narrowing lust for gold." [54] A
part of his vision of "The Golden Year" is of
the time

[50] "The Dawn," p. 888.
[51] *Memoir,* Vol. I, p. 415.
[52] *Ibid.,* p. 396.
[53] *Ibid.,* p. 280.
[54] "In Memoriam," CVI, p. 278.

When wealth no more shall rest in mounded heaps,
But smit with freer light shall slowly melt
In many streams to fatten lower lands,
And light shall spread, and man be liker man.[55]

The division of society into classes results in the corruption and degradation of those possessed of wealth and rank, inducing in them idleness, luxury, and excess. The poor suffer in a different way, but none the less severely. Tennyson has done much to make the sufferings and privations of the poor a reality to the reading and thinking people of England and the world. When Enoch Arden was disabled by an accident, and his income was decreased by the " creeping of another hand across his trade," he saw as in a nightmare his children leading " low, miserable lives of hand-to-mouth," and his beloved wife a beggar.[56] So near to the line of actual want was he compelled to live that, when temporarily disabled, he was in abject fear of beggary. In the cities " the poor are hovell'd and hustled together, each sex, like swine," and have chalk and alum and plaster sold to them for bread.[57] Devitalized by such unhealthful food, and imperiled by conditions of life which make morality all but an impossibility, what wonder that some people say

[55] P. 94.
[56] " Enoch Arden," p. 126.
[57] " Maud," Part I, secs. ix and x, p. 287.

with the Northern Farmer (new style) that " the
poor in a loomp is bad." [58]   This is unjust,
though it is true that some of them do waste their
wages at a pothouse,[59] some steal coal to warm
their window-broken, unsanitary hovels,[60] and
those who become beggars tramp the country,
filch the linen from the hawthorn, poison the
house dogs, and scare lonely maidens at the
farmsteads.[61]   These, however, are the acts of
individuals or of classes among the poor.   Because of such facts as these one has no right to
say that " the poor in a loomp is bad."   On the
contrary,

Plowmen, Shepherds, have I found, and more than
    once, and still could find,
Sons of God, and kings of men in utter nobleness of
    mind.[62]

The condition of a humble milkmaid was not
so hard as to keep Princess Elizabeth from envy-
ing her joys and labors.[63]   This indicates that
life in the country may be more tolerable for the
poor than life in the city.   It shows as well that
the rich and titled have their sorrows and sufferings as certainly as do the poor.   Every condi-

[58] *Poems*, p. 232.
[59] " The Promise of May," Act III, p. 795.
[60] *Ibid.*
[61] " The Foresters," Act III, sc. 1, p. 858.
[62] " Locksley Hall Sixty Years After," p. 563.
[63] " Queen Mary," p. 620.

tion in life has its joys, its delights, and its hardships and griefs. Rich and poor should share each other's burdens and recognize the bonds of a common brotherhood, because of their real kinship to each other and the commonness of the deepest life-experiences.

Tennyson *felt* the hardships of the poor. In the rick-burning days he largely sympathized with the laborers in their demands, though he saw that they were taking the wrong course to accomplish their purpose.[64] The riots of the poorer classes, so far from arousing his disgust and condemnation, only filled him with an earnest desire to do something to help those who lived in misery among the "warrens of the poor."[65] Hallam shared this laudable ambition of his friend, and the two often talked of the wretchedness of the poorer classes which so weighed upon their minds. They appreciated the great difficulty of learning how to remedy these evils, but they determined not to lose hold of the real in seeking the ideal. Hallam wrote: "Where the ideas of time and sorrow are not, and sway not the soul with power, there is no true knowledge in Poetry or Philosophy."[66] In a letter to Aubrey de Vere, written in 1847, Tennyson showed

[64] *Memoir*, Vol. I, p. 41.
[65] *Ibid.*, p. 42.
[66] *Ibid.*, p. 83.

the same sympathetic interest in the poor, and
feared that the bitter weather would be very hard
upon them.[67]   When he visited Ireland at the invitation of this friend, he was greatly shocked
at the poverty of the peasantry and the marks
of havoc wrought in the country by the great
potato famine.[68]   He called upon the poor in his
own vicinage and aided them from his own resources.   The admiration of an old man who
committed his poems to memory because he was
too poor to buy a printed copy, Tennyson reckoned the highest honor he had ever received up
to that time.   Thus throughout his life, by poems
and influence and example, he called to the people
of his land and of every land:

> Ring out the feud of rich and poor,
> Ring in redress to all mankind.[69]

There is nothing to contradict, and much to
support, the belief that it was Tennyson's own
conviction that "ourselves are full of social
wrong." [70]   It becomes men who are awake to
the needs of the time to think earnestly

> How best to help the slender store,
> How mend the dwellings of the poor.[71]

[67] *Ibid.*, p. 261.
[68] *Ibid.*, p. 288.
[69] "In Memoriam," CVI, p. 277.
[70] "The Princess," p. 217.
[71] "To the Rev. F. D. Maurice," p. 234.

how aid the one who " writhes in a world of
the weak trodden down by the strong . . . . a
world all massacre, murder and wrong." [72]
There is still many a son

> who from the wrongs his father did
> Would shape himself a right. [73]

Often " the Higher wields the Lower, while the
Lower is the Higher." [74]   Not only is it true,
as we have already stated, that " city children
soak and blacken soul and sense in city slime,
but also:

> There among the glooming alleys Progress halts on
>   palsied feet,
> Crime and hunger cast our maidens by the thousand on
>   the street.
> There the master scrimps his haggard sempstress of
>   her daily bread,
> There a single sordid attic holds the living and the
>   dead.
> There the smouldering fire of fever creeps across the
>   rotted floor,
> And the crowded couch of incest in the warrens of the
>   poor. [75]

Throughout " Maud " the social evils are portrayed in vivid colors.   The hero in this poem
says that the sins of a nation, which he calls

---

[72] " Despair," p. 545.
[73] " Gareth and Lynette," p. 323.
[74] " Locksley Hall Sixty Years After," p. 563.
[75] *Ibid.*, p. 566.

" civil war," are deadlier in their effect than what
is commonly known as war itself.[76]   With such
conditions existing in the world, we cannot wonder that some cry out against the social order, as,
when the crowd passed the palace in London in
the days of " Queen Mary," the third voice said:
" What am I?   One who cries continually with
sweat and tears to the Lord God that it would
please him out of his infinite love to break down
all kingship and queenship, all priesthood and
prelacy; to cancel and abolish all bonds of human
allegiance, all the magistracy, all the nobles, and
all the wealthy; and to send us again, according
to his promise, the one King, the Christ, and all
things in common, as in the day of the first
church, when Christ Jesus was King.[77]   Edgar,
in " The Promise of May," voices a similar ex-
treme and unwarranted opinion:

> The storm is hard at hand, will sweep away
> Thrones, churches, ranks, traditions, customs,
>   marriage
> One of the feeblest.[78]

Harold, in the same drama, speaks thus:

> What I that have been call'd a Socialist,
> A Communist, a Nihilist — what you will! —
>
> .   .   .   .

[76] *Memoir,* Vol. I, p. 401.
[77] " Queen Mary," Act V, sc. 4, p. 648.
[78] P. 783.

> Utopian idiotcies
> They did not last three Junes. Such rampant weeds
> Strangle each other, die, and make the soil
> For Cæsars, Cromwells, and Napoleons,
> To root their power in. I have freed myself
> From all such dreams, and some will say because
> I have inherited my Uncle.[79]

The ruin wrought by false social ideals, especially that which relates to marriage, is pictured in the closing lines spoken by Dora in "The Promise of May."[80] This is most emphatic condemnation of the false ideals themselves.

Tennyson saw most clearly somber facts, yet his message concerning society is not that of the pessimist. In spite of personal sorrow and social disorder, he says: "I will not shut me from my kind."[81] He hears

> A deeper voice across the storm
> Proclaiming social truth shall spread,
> And justice.[82]

These gloomy facts only impose upon the awakened and enlightened the greater, more solemn obligation to "all live together like brethren."[83] If anyone harms a brother-man,

---

[79] Act III, pp. 800, 801.

[80] P. 803.

[81] "In Memoriam," CVIII, p. 278.

[82] *Ibid.*, CXXVII, p. 283.

[83] "Queen Mary," Act IV, sc. 3, 631.

Albeit he thinks himself at home with God,
Of this be sure, he is whole worlds away.[84]

These luminous words of Cranmer are the words
of Tennyson. Addressing the rich, he says:

You that wanton in affluence,
Spare not now to be bountiful,
Call your poor to regale with you,
All the lowly, the destitute,
Make their neighborhood healthfuller,
Give your gold to the Hospital
Let the weary be comforted,
Let the needy be banqueted,
Let the maimed in his heart rejoice.[85]

It was the noble purpose of Akbar

to fuse his myriads into union under one,
To hunt the tiger of oppression out
From office.[86]

When in town, Tennyson mingled with all
sorts and conditions of men.[87] He appreciated
their aspirations and their needs. The evidences
of social unrest were to him solemn facts to be
diligently studied for the purpose of gaining wisdom for future action. Once, when a member
of a party made a jocular remark about some
disorders apprehended or existing in the centers
of industry, Tennyson solemnly replied: " I

[84] *Ibid.*
[85] " On the Jubilee of Queen Victoria," p. 803.
[86] " Akbar's Dream," p. 881.
[87] *Memoir,* Vol. I, p. 183.

can't joke about so grave a question." [88]   When
visiting with friends, the conversation was often
upon the social difficulties of the time.[89]   He
read "with great pleasure" an account of the
German Ragged Schools as indicating one possible partial solution of the social problem.[90]   His
words are luminous with hope, for he believed
in the presence and power of the Christ-spirit in
the world. He, like his friend J. W. Blakesley,
saw that the cause of the abuses of the present
system is the selfish spirit which pervades the
whole frame of society. He knew that, if the
effects are to be banished, the cause must be removed.[91]

To accomplish so great a work, the Christ,
"the strong Son of God, Immortal Love," alone
is sufficient. What he can do is indicated by
what he has done. When a friend once spoke of
Christ as an example of failure, he replied: "Do
you call that failure which has altered the belief
and the social relations of the whole world?"[92]
He saw this great ideal of the Christ leading individuals and the world on to the conquest of the
selfishness which corrupts and destroys. In

[88] *Memoir,* Vol. I, p. 205.
[89] *Ibid.,* p. 468.
[90] *Ibid.,* p. 512.
[91] *Ibid.,* p. 69.
[92] *Ibid.,* p. 512.

" The Voyage " the thought is put in figure, but it is his thought none the less:

> But, blind or lame or sick or sound,
>   We follow that which flies before;
> We know the merry world is round,
>   And we may sail for evermore.[93]

The spirit of the Christ flies before, and those who follow will leave behind the selfishness which degrades, and ever approach the love which exalts and purifies and frees the individual and the world.

[93] *Poems,* p. 118.

CHAPTER VII

SOCIAL INSTITUTIONS: THE STATE, THE CHURCH

As society comes to self-consciousness, certain ideas which are held in common by members of the social group find expression in institutions. These are of great service in registering the thought-progress of a people, and in making prominent and efficient the ideas which might otherwise lie buried in the minds of men. Institutions are the hands with which ideas do their work. These are the bodies of which ideas are the spirit and life. They deserve reverence because of the work they do and the spirit they enshrine. They have no power in themselves. They are the channels through which ideas flow to act upon the world.

By their very nature institutions are subject to change. Truth is constant and unchanging, but the individual and social apprehension of truth grows and develops. Falsehoods are removed. Useless or outworn theories are discarded. An institution can express only that part or phase of truth which those who create or sustain it have apprehended. As the ideas of people grow, the form of their expression must change. Likewise, as the needs which an institution exists to meet vary, there must be a corresponding change in that which was created to meet the needs. When the idea or the need entirely passes away, the institution must decay or be abolished.

These great social truths Tennyson has expressed with clearness and beauty. " Morte D'Arthur " has the same meaning essentially as the " Passing of Arthur." Arthur, the pure soul of man, passes, while the Round Table, with its knights and tournaments and quests, the institutions of men, decay and disappear. In these great poems Bedivere represents the conservative spirit so in love with the sword Excalibur, a mere instrument for the conquest of Arthur's foes, that it is exceedingly hard for him to part with it even at the command of the king. He looks upon its wondrous beauty, thinks of all it has wrought through the might of the king, and cannot bear to have it lost to the world. After two fruitless attempts to hurl it into the sea, as Arthur commanded, the third time he succeeds, closing his eyes lest the glittering gems should again conquer his purpose to obey the dying king.

" Sea Dreams " is akin to this in thought. The swelling wave represents essential, absolute truth. Men in their imaginings have built cathedrals with statues of saints and martyrs. The wave swells and destroys these forms, threatening even the most sacred images. Arthur passes, but comes again in a higher and diviner form. Institutions fail, and truth passes on in other and nobler creations. In general, he teaches that all things subject to physical evolution are subject to destruction and decay. " De Profundis " is notable among other things, for its expression of this thought. This poem is a significant comment upon " The Idylls." The Round Table, and all institutions subject to physical evolution, are liable to destruction. The Arthurs are births out of the spirit, and pass, to come again in ever higher and higher forms.

I.   THE STATE

One of the great social institutions of which Tennyson speaks with special interest and enthusiasm is the state. He has no new or startling theory of government to exploit. He does not expressly declare his own preference for any detailed system of government. Rather, as an English patriot, he writes of his own state, her statesmen, throne, empire, and political problems. He may almost be said to take it for granted that the English government is the best in the world. This would not be exactly true, however; for his loyalty to his own land is not unintelligent. He, knows what other governments are, and what they have accomplished for their people. He had read history with interest and profit. He was a careful observer of the political movements of his time. Yet, after all his reading and study and observation he came back to view his own England with renewed satisfaction. He boasts of England as the land of settled government, as contrasted with France, where

> The gravest citizen seems to lose his head,
> The king is scared, the soldiers will not fight,
> The little boys begin to shoot and stab,
> A kingdom topples over with a shriek
> Like an old woman, and down rolls the world
> In mock heroics stranger than our own;
> Revolts, republics, revolutions, most
> No graver than a school boys' barring out;
> Too comic for the solemn things they are,
> Too solemn for the comic touches in them.[1]

In the " Ode on the Death of the Duke of Wellington " these lines occur, referring to the same country :

> A people's voice! We are a people yet,
> Tho' all men else their nobler dreams forget,
> Confused by brainless mobs and lawless Powers.[2]

In " The Third of February " he says:

> We love not this French God, the child of Hell,
> Wild War who breaks the converse of the wise.[3]

[1] " The Princess," p. 217.
[2] Sec. 7, p. 219.
[3] P. 221.

As one of the " signs of storm " he speaks of
" Art with poisonous honey stol'n from France." [4]
Equally significant lines occur in " Locksley Hall
Sixty Years After ":

France had shown a light to all men, preach'd a Gospel,
   All men's good;
Celtic Demos rose a Demon, shriek'd and slaked the
   light with blood.[5]

Paris was to him " the centre and crater of European confusion." [6] As a young man he spent
some time in France, but never became an enthusiastic admirer of the French character. He
said: " I am struck on returning from France
with the look of good sense in the London people." [7] The reader may draw his own inference
as to the poet's opinion of the looks of the Pari-
sians. Tennyson quotes John Kemble's phrase,
" the moral barbarism of France," as if it were
worth repeating for the truth it contains, and this
barbarism was manifested in the affairs of state
as perhaps nowhere else.

   Emily Tennyson was in Paris in 1848, after
the revolution against Louis Philippe had begun.
She was shot at by one of the revolutionists, as
she was looking out of the window. The bullet

---

[4] " To the Queen," p. 475.
[5] P. 562.
[6] " Beautiful City," p. 835.
[7] *Memoir*, Vol. I, p. 55.

missed her, but went through the ceiling. She wrote home an account of these stormy days, and this doubtless strengthened Tennyson's aversion to the fickle forms of government for which the French are famous.[8] He was the voice of those who regarded France under Napoleon as a serious menace to the peace of Europe. But in the later years, after the Franco-German War, he expressed great admiration for the dignified way in which France gradually recovered herself. The France that was charmed only by martial prowess he could not praise. It was " the wiser France " he lauded. Such a nation, he believed, would work with England for the good of the world and hasten the coming of the universal brotherhood.[9]

This reference to France and the French government is in place here because of the emphasis it gives to Tennyson's opinion of what the state should *not* be. He did not, could not, applaud " phantoms of other forms of rule " that were " vague in vapour, hard to mark." [10] He believed in

> our slowly-grown
> And crown'd Republic's crowning common-sense.[11]

[8] *Ibid.*, pp. 272 f.
[9] *Ibid.*, pp. 344, 380.
[10] " Love Thou Thy Land," p. 65.
[11] " To the Queen," p. 475.

He called England a republic, a "crowned republic," and believed in the saving common-sense
of her people. Every state may have at times
weak, corrupt, or inefficient officials. Then it is
the duty of the ruler to follow the example of
Arthur, who

> Rooted out the slothful officer
> Or guilty, which for bribe had wink'd at wrong,
> And in their chairs set up a stronger race
> With hearts and hands, and sent a thousand men
> To till the wastes, and moving everywhere
> Clear'd the dark places and let in the law.[12]

The court must be pure and strong, or enemies
will be triumphant and the land will suffer. The
sinful, conscience-smitten queen, fleeing to Almes-
bury from the ruin she had wrought, says:

> For now the heathen of the Northern Sea,
> Lured by the crimes and frailties of the court,
> Begin to slay the folk, and spoil the land.[13]

The great-hearted king himself realized the cause
of his downfall and cried: "My house hath
been my doom;" though he would not call
Modred the traitor of his house.[14] The downfall
of Queen Mary is in part explained by these
words of Bagenhall:

[12] "Geraint and Enid," pp. 368, 369.
[13] "Guinevere," p. 458.
[14] "The Passing of Arthur," p. 469.

We have no men among us. The new Lords
Are quieted with their sop of Abbeylands,
And ev'n before the Queen's face Gardiner buys
    them
With Philip's gold. All greed, no faith, no courage.[15]

Tennyson never believed and never taught

that lying
And ruling men are fatal twins that cannot
Move one without the other,[16]

but rather counseled honesty, purity, and truth
in ruler and court. The opposite of these are
among the sins of a nation that are deadlier than
war.[17] The *Idylls of the King* are the poet's
statement of the high aim that every state should
constantly cherish. These poems show as certainly that, when a government fails to accomplish that purpose which is at the same time political and spiritual, it is not primarily because of
misfortune, or of some attack from without, but
because of moral evil that overthrows the very
foundations of the state.[18] One of the highest
encomiums pronounced upon the queen was that
" her court was pure." [19]

It is plain that England's hereditary monarchy

---

[15] " Queen Mary," Act III, sc. 1, p. 605.
[16] " Harold," Act III, p. 672.
[17] *Memoir*, Vol. I, p. 401.
[18] *Ibid.*, p. 511.
[19] " To the Queen," p. 1.

was the " crowned republic " that the poet commended. He does not desire a change from a hereditary to an elected ruler. He writes " To the Queen " :

> May you rule us long,
> And leave us rulers of your blood
> As noble till the latest day ! [20]

He sounded the alarm of Tiresias,

> that the tyranny of one
> Was prelude to the tyranny of all.

He repeated the warning,

> that the tyranny of all
> Led backward to the tyranny of one. [21]

In " Hands All Round " these lines occur, showing his desire for a large-minded policy on the part of the houses of Parliament, and of the people who gave them power :

> To both our Houses may they see
> Beyond the borough and the shire !
> We sail'd wherever ship could sail,
> We founded many a mighty state;
> Pray God our greatness may not fail,
> Thro' craven fears of being great. [22]

He believed with all his heart in the larger England. He was careful to say that wherever the

---

[20] *Loc. cit.*

[21] " Tiresias," p. 539.

[22] P. 575.

British flag went, there were his fellow-citizens, his "brethren;" there was an opportunity to make men milder by just government.[23]

> Wisdom when in power
> And wisest, should not frown as Power, but smile
> As Kindness, watching all, till the true *must*
> Shall make her strike as Power.[24]

> Traitors are rarely bred
> Save under traitor kings.[25]

He was ever the herald and advocate of liberty, and this involved hatred of a tyrant king or of a tyrant majority. Government is but a channel through which to convey the people's wishes.[26]

Victoria was to him the ideal sovereign of English people. What he says of her he says with a feeling of loyal affection and of patriotic pride. The tributes which he paid to the queen were not the servile, mechanical laudations of a hired man of the crown. They were the sincere expressions of a genuine admirer and loyal subject. His loyalty was chivalrous and ardent. He believed that

> She wrought her people lasting good;
> Her court was pure, her life serene;
> God gave her peace; her land reposed;

[23] "Harold," Act I, sc. 1, p. 656.
[24] *Ibid.*
[25] "The Foresters," Act II, p. 847.
[26] *Memoir,* Vol. I, p. 111.

A thousand claims to reverence closed
In her as Mother, Wife, and Queen;
And statesmen at her council met
Who knew the seasons when to take
Occasion by the hand, and make
The bounds of freedom wider yet
By shaping some august decree,
Which kept her throne unshaken still,
Broad-based upon her people's will,
And compass'd by the inviolate sea.[27]

There can be no reasonable doubt that such tributes helped to make steady the foundation of the British throne. He gave expression to the loyalty of the common people, that might otherwise have been voiceless.

In various other ways does he portray his ideal of the ruler of a realm. Arthur, in a sense, stands as the model king, though he failed through the treachery and sin of some whom he had chosen. The true sovereign will be loved by the people. For Victoria he prayed: "The love of all thy people comfort thee."[28] So Arthur was held in honor and affection by all the knights of the round table. Even Mary recognized "love as one of the strongest bonds uniting ruler and people."[29] Elizabeth likewise loved the people and felt confident of their love for

[27] "To the Queen," p. 1.
[28] "Dedication," p. 388.
[29] "Queen Mary," Act II, sc. 2, p. 598.

her.[30]   The power which a ruler has over those whom he loves and governs was thus expressed by Robin:

> I believe their lives
> No man who truly loves and truly rules
> His following, but can keep his followers true.[31]

That such love could be expressed Akbar believed. He declared that kings should show a warmth of love for all they rule, and give to them equal law and deeds that shall be a light to men.[32] Arthur, the ideal king, was honored and loved by the people as well as by his knights. He unified all the petty princedoms and reigned over them as one realm.[33]   His power was not maintained by the display of riches or of royal symbols.

> He neither wore on helm or shield
> The golden symbol of his knighthood,
> But rode a simple knight among his knights,
> And many of these in richer arms than he.[34]

He was not motived by a selfish ambition, but showed that in spirit he was worthy to rule over a people aspiring to

[30] *Ibid.*, Act V, sc. 3, p. 646.
[31] "The Foresters," Act II, sc. 1, p. 847.
[32] "Akbar's Dream," p. 880.
[33] "The Coming of Arthur," p. 309.
[34] *Ibid.*

Have power on this dark land to lighten it,
And power on this dead world to make it live. [35]

Gareth recognized in him a true king, because he won freedom for the people.

Who should be king save him
Who makes us free? [36]

he asks. When one who had hated the king came to him for help in her distress, Arthur answered:

We sit king, to help the wrong'd
Thro' all our realm. [37]

He was never indifferent to the sufferings of others, though he did condemn himself

As one that let foul wrong stagnate and be,
By having look'd too much thro' alien eyes,
And wrought too long with delegated hands,
Not used mine own. [38]

He felt the kingdom had a rightful claim upon him and all his possessions. Even the jewels of the crown which he had snatched from the tarn he declared belonged not to the king, but to the kingdom for public use. Hence he decreed that that there should be once every year a joust for one of these precious diamonds. [39]

---

[35] *Loc. cit.*, p. 310.
[36] "Gareth and Lynette," p. 319.
[37] *Ibid.*, p. 323.
[38] "Geraint and Enid," p. 363.
[39] "Lancelot and Elaine," p. 396.

There were some who could not appreciate such nobleness as this. Guinevere called him " a moral child without the craft to rule." [40] He did not leave his realm to follow wandering fires, knowing —

> That the king must guard
> That which he rules, and is but as the hind
> To whom a space of land is given to plow.
> Who may not wander from the allotted field
> Before his work be done; but being done,
> Let visions of the night or of the day
> Come, as they will. [41]

The ruler and his people become really one through their loyal love the one for the other, as husband and wife are one in the bonds of wedded love. It is Arthur, the ideal king, who says:

> The king who fights his people, fights himself.
> And they my knights, who loved me once, the stroke
> That strikes them dead is as my death to me. [42]

Queen Mary knew enough of what should be to talk of loving her people and being loved by them. But this love was to her a name rather than a reality. She defied her council, her people, her parliament, in order to carry out a cherished plan of her own. [43]

Freedom loathes such a lawless ruler even as

[40] *Ibid.*, p. 398.
[41] " The Holy Grail," p. 433.
[42] " The Passing of Arthur," p. 468.
[43] " Queen Mary," Act I, sc. 5, p. 588.

she loathes a lawless crowd.[44] It may be true
that

> To sit high
> Is to be lied about,[45]

but it is the duty of the ruler to see that the truth
commends his action toward his people. William the Conqueror promised to rule the domain
upon which he was soon to enter according to the
laws of the land, and make the

> ever-jarring Earldoms move
> To music and in order.[46]

Henry II, who sought to compel Becket to sign
the ancient laws and customs of the realm, was
a lawless king, who represented the tyrant's
power without a kingly love for his subjects.[47]
Such a despot cannot feel with the free.[48] These
abusers of royal power, as they are portrayed
in the lines of Tennyson, really add luster to the
name of Arthur, the ideal king, to whom the poet
dared to compare Albert, the prince consort, and
Victoria, the feminine counterpart of the mighty
head of the table round.

> The noblest men methinks are bred
> Of ours, the Saxo-Norman race,

[44] " Freedom," p. 576.
[45] " Queen Mary," Act I, sc. 5, p. 592.
[46] " Harold," Act II, sc. 2, pp. 670, 692.
[47] " Becket," Act I, sc. 3, p. 704.
[48] " Riflemen Form," p. 890.

> And in the world the noblest place,
> Madam, is yours, our queen and head.[49]

What has already been said shows that in government the statesman stands next to the ruler. One evidence of the wisdom of a monarch is his choice of wise counselors. The Duke of Wellington is praised by the poet as a statesman as well as a warrior. He is commended as moderate, resolute, unselfish, wise, simple, rich in saving common-sense.[50] He was not of the number of those who betray their party secret to the press.[51] Prince Albert was another noble and able statesman who never made "his high place the lawless perch of wing'd ambitions, nor a vantage ground for pleasure."[52] He labored for the people, especially for the poor, and summoned war and waste "to fruitful strifes and rivalries of peace."[53] The lines "To the Duke of Argyll"[54] give a fairly complete picture of what the statesman should be. These declare in poetic form what could not be made clearer by the most prosaic analysis:

[49] *Memoir,* Vol. I, "Dedication;" an unpublished version of "To the Queen," 1851.
[50] *Poems,* p. 220.
[51] "Maud," V, 3, p. 305.
[52] "Dedication of Idylls," p. 308.
[53] *Ibid.*
[54] P. 575.

> O Patriot Statesman, be thou wise to know
> The limits of resistance, and the bounds
> Determining concession; still be bold
> Not only to slight praise but suffer scorn;
> And be thy heart a fortress to maintain
> The day against the moment, and the year
> Against the day; thy voice, a music heard
> Thro' all the yells and counter yells of feud
> And faction, and thy will, a power to make
> This ever-changing world of circumstance,
> In changing chime with never-changing Law.

Such a statesman will be a " true leader of the land's desires." [55]   He will not " jeer and fleer at men," thus making enemies for himself and for the king.[56]   He will take " Truth herself for model," [57] though he be familiar with the old saying:

> That were a man of state nakedly true,
> Men would but take him for the craftier liar.[58]

Such a man will be the confidant of the king, for

> State secrets should be patent to the statesman
> Who serves and loves his king.[59]

He once said of Blakesley: " He ought to be Lord Chancellor, for he is a subtle and powerful

---

[55] " Hands All Round," p. 575.
[56] " Queen Mary," Act II, sc. 2, p. 601.
[57] *Ibid.*, Act III, sc. 3, p. 612.
[58] " Harold," Act III, sc. 1, p. 672.
[59] " Becket," Prologue," p. 694.

reasoner, and an honest man." [60]   As early as 1833 he cursed " O'Connell for as double-dyed a rascal as ever was dipped in the Styx of political villainy," but his son informs us that he softened this opinion when he came to know more about the Irish statesman.[61]

He believed that a poet, while ardently loving his own country, should write of what is noble and great in the history of all countries.   His utterances should be outspoken, yet statesmanlike and without narrow partisanship.[62]   As an illustration of what he conceived such an utterance should be, it is worth while to quote a few lines from an unpublished poem of the 1831–33 period :

> For where is he, the citizen,
> Deep-hearted, moderate, firm, who sees
> His path before him?   Not with these,
> Shadows of statesmen, clever men !
>
> Uncertain of ourselves we chase
> The clap of hands, we jar like boys:
> And in the hurry and the noise
> Great spirits grow akin to base.
>
> .   .   .   .
>
> Ill fares a people passion-wrought,
> A land of many days that cleaves

[60] *Memoir*, Vol. I, p. 38.
[61] *Ibid.*, p. 101.
[62] *Ibid.*, pp. 209, 210.

In two great halves, when each one leaves
The middle road of sober thought.

Not he that breaks the dams, but he
That thro' the channels of the state
Convoys the people's wish, is great;
His name is pure, his fame is free;

He cares, if ancient usage fade,
To shape, to settle, to repair,
With seasonable changes fair,
And innovation grade by grade:

Or, if the sense of most require
A precedent of larger scope,
Not deals in threats, but works with hope,
And lights at length on his desire,

Knowing those laws are just alone
That contemplate a mighty plan,
The frame, the mind, the soul of man,
Like one that cultivates his own.

He seeing far an end sublime,
Contends, despising party-rage,
To hold the Spirit of the Age
Against the Spirit of the Time.[63]

One important means by which government seeks to accomplish its beneficent purpose for society is law. This thought is really related to the poet's conception of evolution. He believed

[63] *Memoir*, Vol. I, pp. 110, 111.

that bodies develop in accordance with a law
which is within themselves.   This law cannot
be annihilated by human intelligence, but may be
concretely stated by one who has gained a knowledge of its operations.   It is the part of the individual to give ready obedience to that law which
is within himself and which may be stated in
scientific language.   The social body has laws
of its own which are within itself, and all its
development takes place in accordance with these
internal principles.   It is the work of the statesman and the legislator to learn what these laws
are and give to them worthy expression.   It is
the part of the public servant to demand obedience to these,. and the part of the individual to
render the obedience demanded.   Then the normal, the practical idea of " ruling " is " by obey-
ing nature's powers." [64]   Law is universal.
There is and can be no exception.   " Nothing is
that errs from law." [65]   This is not to be be-
wailed as a calamity.   It is our wisdom

> To live by law,
> Acting the law we live by without fear.[66]

Anyone who has eyes to see may see

> The hollow orb of moving circumstance
> Roll'd round by one fix'd law.[67]

[64] " International Exhibition Ode," p. 223.
[65] " In Memoriam," LXXIII, p. 265.
[66] " Ænone," p. 42.
[67] " The Palace of Art," p. 48.

The Princess declares, with a wisdom greater than she knows:

> All things serve their time
> Toward that great year of equal mights and rights,
> Nor would I fight with iron laws, in the end
> Found golden.[68]

With man as he is, it is not sufficient merely to " hold by the law within." [69] That law must have external expression, and must be obeyed if it is to be efficient in securing the development of the individual and of society. The wise man will discern the proper time in which to express that inner principle in human legislation, " and in its season bring the law." [70]

Our knowledge of these inner and external laws, written in the very constitution of man and of society, is of course imperfect. Consequently, our expression of them can only be partial and incomplete. This may lead either to an overestimate or an underestimate of law.

> God is law, say the wise; O Soul, and let us rejoice,
> For if he thunder by law the thunder is yet his voice.
> Law is God, say some; no God at all, says the fool;
> For all we have power to see is a straight staff bent
>   in a pool.[71]

[68] " The Princess, p. 187.
[69] " In Memoriam," XXXIII, p. 256.
[70] *Poems*, p. 65.
[71] " The Higher Pantheism," p. 239.

The imperfection of our knowledge of the eternal laws which it is the business of the statesman to discover and embody in statute is not at all to be wondered at. Progress, evolution, is the method here as everywhere. As we find errors in the legislation of the past, these can be corrected, and the new truth discerned can be incorporated into other laws. This should teach us

Some reverence for the laws ourselves have made,
Some patient force to change them when we will.[72]

When the laws are broken with impunity, the doom of the realm is sealed. The breaking of the laws of the Tournament, without a word from the great umpire, proclaimed the real destruction and decay of the Round Table.[73] A lawless realm is a broken realm. There the wrongs of the weak and defenseless go unavenged.[74] If the laws are cruel, they should be changed until they are just.[75] If to some who have suffered it seems that " the lawyer is born but to murder," [76] that

often justice drowns
Between the law and letter of the law,[77]

[72] " The Princess," p. 216.
[73] " The Last Tournament," p. 446.
[74] " Geraint and Enid," p. 362.
[75] " Becket," Act V, sc. 2, p. 741.
[76] " Rizpah," p. 503.
[77] " The Foresters," Act IV, sc. 1, p. 866.

it is to be remembered that these are defects in
" the lawless science,of our law " [78] and in administration.   These are defects that may be removed
in time.   England's government already stands
for justice, not for hollow form.   The justiciary
in " The Foresters " says:

> If the king
> Condemn us without trial, men will call him
> An Eastern tyrant, not an English king.[79]

Government in England, the poet believes, stands
for justice, for " equal law for all." [80]   This condition in the poet's land is prophetic of the time
when

> The common sense of most shall hold a fretful realm
>   in Awe,
> And the kindly earth shall slumber, lapt in universal
>   law.[81]

This conception of law in government expressly provides for changes that are in the nature of innovations.   He believed that the new
in government should be so joined with the old
as to make one system.   Progress to him did not
mean a break with the past, but simply an advance.

[78] " Aylmer's Field," p. 149.
[79] Act IV, sc. 1, p. 870.
[80] " Akbar's Dream," p. 880.
[81] " Locksley Hall," p. 101.

So let the change which comes be free
To ingroove itself with that which flies,
And work, a joint of state, that plies
Its office, moved with sympathy.

. . . .

Of many changes, aptly joined,
Is bodied forth the second whole.
Regard gradation, lest the soul
Of Discord race the rising wind.

. . . .

Tomorrow yet would reap today,
As we bear blossom of the dead;
Earn well the thrifty months, nor wed
Raw Haste, half sister to Delay.[82]

A similar expression of this same opinion occurs in " The Statesman," a part of which has been already quoted.

He cares, if ancient usage fade,
To shape, to settle, to repair,
With seasonable changes fair,
And innovation grade by grade.[83]

Arthur recognized that changes are needful to the progress of the world, and said:

The old order changeth, yielding place to new,
And God fulfils himself in many ways,
Lest one good custom should corrupt the world.[84]

The same great truth is taught by " Freedom ":

---

[82] " Love Thou Thy Land," pp. 65, 66.
[83] *Memoir,* Vol. I, p. 111.
[84] " The Passing of Arthur," p. 473.

Who yet, like Nature, wouldst not mar
By changes all too fierce and fast
This order of Her Human Star
This heritage of the past.[85]

Innovations in government and society are to be expected and desired. These, however, should be vitally related to the past, and should prepare the way for a higher form of individual and associated life in the future.

In every government there are some who stand as advocates of innovation, and some who oppose the new and cling tenaciously to the old. This has naturally resulted in the formation of parties. Parties have been subdivided into factions, actuated by selfish motives and seeking, not the good of the state, but the accomplishment of unworthy ends. Tennyson calls the members of these cliques " dogs of Faction." [86] He gave high praise to Prince Albert as one " not swaying to this faction or to that." [87] Similar commendation is given to the Duke of Argyll, whose voice was

a music heard
Through all the yells and counter yells of feud
And faction.[88]

[85] P. 576.
[86] *Poems,* p. 66.
[87] " Dedication of Idylls," p. 308.
[88] " To the Duke of Argyll," p. 575.

Such factions are inevitably dangerous to the state, for they seek, not the good of the many, but the selfish aggrandizement of the few.

True freedom is a

> Scorner of the party cry,
> That wanders from the public good.[89]

" Locksley Hall Sixty Years After " contains one line that gives special emphasis to the danger from this source:

Nay, but these would feel and follow Truth, if only you and you,
Rivals of realm-ruining party, when you speak were wholly true.[90]

Tennyson loved Freedom for her own sake and was, " wed to no faction in the state." [91] More than that, he was of the number of those " who loathed parties and sects," [92] like the statesman he describes, " despising party-rage." [93] He believed that, if there were more of a partiotic and less of a party spirit in the press, the Chartist and socialist agitation could be more easily met; so [94] he cries in the unpublished poem " Jack Tar ": " the d—l take the parties." [95]

[89] " Freedom," p. 576.
[90] P. 563.
[91] *Memoir*, Vol. I, p. 41.
[92] *Ibid.*, p. 42.
[93] *Ibid.*, p. 111.
[94] *Ibid.*, p. 185.
[95] *Ibid.*, p. 437.

One of the great perils of factional agitations is that these may lead to the violence of revolt or revolution. The history of the French people reveals the unfortunate results of such disturbances of the social order. What has already been said concerning France is sufficient to show the poet's attitude toward what is distinctive in the government of that country. He called Bonaparte " madman," [96] and in " Aylmer's Field " he speaks of " that cursed France with her egalities." [97] There was a time when there were many who, like Wordsworth, " had golden hopes for France and all mankind;" [98] but Tennyson was always suspicious of the permanence of a progress attained by such means as the French people employed. As early as 1842 he asked:

O shall the braggart shout,
For some blind glimpse of freedom work itself,
Thro' madness, hated by the wise, to law,
System and empire? [99]

Those who had cherished the " golden hopes for France " were doomed to bitter disappointment. This was the keener because of the great promise of light which the earlier days had given:

[96] " Buonaparte," p. 25.
[97] P. 146.
[98] *Ibid.*, p. 149.
[99] " Love and Duty," ^ 92.

France had shown a light to all men, preach'd a Gospel,
    All men's good;
Celtic Demos rose a Demon, shriek'd and slaked the
    light with blood.[100]

This brings chaos, confusion, and disaster, in which is " freedom, free to slay herself, and dying while they shout her name." [101] Liberty and progress are not honored, they are destroyed, by such defiance of the past and of the great laws of social development. The wise man will

                             maintain
    The day against the moment, and the year
    Against the day,[102]

not " expecting all things in an hour." [103]

When tyrants are in power, abuses are suffered, but such revolutions as France has known are likely only to add new and even greater calamities. In the lines entitled " Beautiful City," he says:

Beautiful city, the centre and crater of European
    confusion,
O you with your passionate shriek for the rights of an
    equal humanity,
How often your Re-volution has proven but E-volution

---

[100] " Locksley Hall Sixty Years After," p. 562.
[101] *Ibid.,* p. 563.
[102] " To the Duke of Argyll," p. 575.
[103] " Freedom," X, p. 576.

Roll'd again back on itself in the tides of a civic
insanity.[104]

This is one of the poems corroborative of the
statement of the younger Tennyson concerning
his illustrious father: " Indeed from first to last
he always preached the onward progress of
liberty, while steadily opposed to revolutionary
license." [105]   He and Hallam started for the Pyr-
enees with money for the insurgent allies of Tor-
rijos, a noble, accomplished, truthful leader, who
raised the standard of revolt against the Inquisi-
tion and the tyranny of Ferdinand, king of Spain.
This bit of practice was entirely in accord with
his preaching. He hated tyranny and oppression; he loved liberty and right. Liberty once
gained, however, he believed should be maintained, and innovations should be introduced
" grade by grade."

II. THE CHURCH

Tennyson looked upon the church as one of
the great institutions of organized society. He
studied it with care and sympathy, and wrote of
it with wisdom and power. He believed that
the church exists to meet a real social need, and
that its maintenance is a civic and patriotic duty.
The fundamental fact upon which the church is
based, and which makes it a permanent necessity,

[104] P. 835.
[105] *Memoir*, Vol. I, p. 42.

is " an Omnipotent, Omni-present and All-loving
God, who has revealed himself through the human attribute of the highest self-sacrificing
love." [106]   In all the affairs of life, " there is a
hand that guides." [107]

> Closer is He than breathing,
> And nearer than hands and feet.[108]

His are

> the hands
> That reach through nature, moulding men.[109]

In all of the sufferings of the individual, in all
of the bewilderments of the world, in all of the
struggles of class against class in human society,
in all the jealousies and wars between nations,
the individual should comfort himself with the
thought : " I have not made the world, and He
that made it will guide." [110]   There are times
of darkness and of seeming failure, when even
the noble Arthur says :

> I found Him in the shining of the stars,
> I marked Him in the flowering of His fields,
> But in His ways with men, I find Him not.[111]

Yet, in the same breath he suggests an explana-

[106] *Ibid.*, p. 311.
[107] " The Princess," p. 217.
[108] " The Higher Pantheism," p. 239.
[109] " In Memoriam," CXXIV, p. 283.
[110] " Maud," IV, 8, p. 290.
[111] " The Passing of Arthur," p. 467.

tion of this seeming absence of God from " the ways of men " :

> These eyes of men are dense and dim,
> And have not power to see it as it is.

With unfailing faith he declares, I shall

> learn that Love which is, and was
> My Father and my Brother and my God.[112]

Confident of this future knowledge, he says in his lines " On the Jubilee of Queen Victoria " :

> Are there thunders moaning in the distance?
> Are there spectres moving in the darkness?
> Trust, the Hand of Light, will lead her people,
> Till the thunders pass, the spectres vanish,
> And the Light is Victor, and the darkness
> Dawns into the Jubilee of the Ages.[113]

If God is in the world as a God of wisdom and of love, guiding the affairs of men, and giving to all his two great commandments of love to God and love to brother-men, religion, or the recognition of God as an object of worship, love, and obedience, is a perfectly natural phenomenon in human society. When men have false ideas of the character of God and of his requirements, superstitions and wrong systems of worship arise. The search for the Holy Grail by the Knights of the Round Table degenerated into asceticism and

---

[112] " Doubt and Prayer," p. 891.
[113] Pp. 805, 806.

a religion of sense. Arthur found service in fields near at hand. Galahad, by purity and self-sacrifice, was able to gain a sight of the Holy Grail. The service rendered by Arthur and that by Galahad were not essentially different. Enoch Arden would have died of solitude,

> had not his poor heart
> Spoken with That, which being everywhere,
> Lets none who speaks with Him seem all alone.[114]

Edith, in "Aylmer's Field," is described as one,

> Not sowing hedgerow texts and passing by,
> Nor dealing goodly counsel from a height
> That makes the lowest hate it, but a voice
> Of comfort and an open hand of help,
> A splendid presence flattering the poor roofs,
> Revered as theirs, but kindlier than themselves
> To ailing wife or wailing infancy
> Or old bedridden palsy.[115]

King Arthur said to his knights:

> This chance of noble deeds will come and go
> Unchallenged, while ye follow wandering fires,
> Lost in the quagmire.[116]

When the Holy Grail actually appeared upon a beam of light,

> Every knight beheld his fellow's face,
> As in a glory.[117]

[114] "Enoch Arden," p. 134.
[115] P. 145.
[116] "The Holy Grail," p. 423.
[117] *Ibid.*, p. 421.

It is the practical idea of religion which is also embodied in the words of " The Village Wife " :

But I beänt that sewer es the Lord, howsiver they
    praäy'd an' praäy'd,
Lets them inter 'eaven eäsy es leäves their debts do be
    paäid.[118]

The poem " Despair " was based upon the following incident, which appealed strongly to the poet. Loss of faith in God and immortality caused a man and his wife, who were utterly miserable in this life, to resolve to end themselves by drowning. The woman was drowned, but the man was rescued by a minister of the sect he had abandoned. The poem expresses the despair of a soul from whom faith in God has departed. Dora, in " The Promise of May," quotes her mother as saying that

                    a soul with no religion —
Was without rudder, anchor, compass — might be,
Blown everyway with every gust and wreck
On any rock.[119]

In the notes to " Akbar's Dream " [120] Tennyson speaks thus of the great Mogul Emperor Akbar : " His tolerance of religions and his abhorrence of religious persecution put our Tudors to shame.

[118] P. 516.
[119] Act III, p. 800.
[120] P. 882.

He invented a new eclectic religion by which he hoped to unite all creeds, castes and peoples; and his legislation was remarkable for vigour, justice and humanity." Tennyson exalted the religion of tolerance, of unselfish service, and of brotherly love. He spoke of the follies of formalism and ritualism only to ridicule and condemn them. It was the truth in religion that he sought and exalted and proclaimed. That he was a close and careful student of the Bible, his writings abundantly attest. Yet he was more than this. He recognized that there are great and fundamental truths which underlie all religions, and these he sought and studied with special interest. As a result of all his thought and investigations, he declared his agreement with Maurice that " all religions seemed to him to be imperfect manifestations of the true Christianity." [121]

Of Christianity he said: " It is rugging at my heart." [122] It would be difficult to find anyone in all modern literature who has grasped more firmly and expressed more clearly the conviction that " Christianity is Christ," than has Alfred Tennyson. He believed in the power of the creed that Christ lived.

[121] *Memoir,* Vol. I, p. 431.
[122] *Ibid.,* p. 264.

And so the word had breath, and wrought
With human hands the creed of creeds
In loveliness of perfect deeds,
More strong than all poetic thought.[123]

Throughout his life he read with unfailing interest " the teaching of Christ, that purest light of God." [124]   He believed that the greatest and best work of the world had been accomplished under the inspiration of his life and teaching. The nurse " In the Children's Hospital " says:

O how could I serve in the wards, if the hope of the world were a lie?
How could I bear with the sights and the loathsome smells of disease,
But that He said, " ye do it to me, when ye do it to these ? " [125]

When Telemachus flung himself into the arena and stood between the gladiatorial swords, he called:

Forbear, in the great name of him who died for men,
Christ Jesus! [126]

On one occasion, before referred to, when a friend spoke of Christ as an example of failure, the poet replied: " Do you call that failure which has altered the belief and the social rela-

[123] " In Memoriam," XXXVI, p. 257.
[124] *Memoir,* Vol. I, p. 169.
[125] P. 517.
[126] " St. Telemachus," p. 878.

tions of the whole world?" [127] He realized that the true Christ is now only very imperfectly understood, and his teaching and life very imperfectly followed. He looked for a more complete knowledge of him and a more perfect society, as he becomes an increasing power in the world. He cried over and over again: "Ring in the Christ that is to be." [128] One of his purposes in this line, he said, is to herald the time when Christianity without bigotry will triumph, when the controversies of creeds shall have vanished, and

> Shall bear false witness each of each no more
> But find their limits by that larger light,
> And overstep them, moving easily
> Thro' after-ages in the love of Truth,
> The truth of Love.[129]

This is Arthur come again to earth, and welcomed by all the people, who cry:

> Come,—
> With all good things, and war shall be no more.[130]

Then he adds these significant closing words:

> At this a hundred bells began to peal,
> That with the sound I woke, and heard indeed,
> The clear church bells ring in the Christmas-morn.[131]

[127] *Memoir,* Vol. I, p. 512.
[128] " In Memoriam," CVI, p. 278.
[129] *Memoir,* Vol. I, p. 326.
[130] " Morte D'Arthur," p. 72.
[131] *Ibid.*

Of the details of church organization and government the poet, of course, does not treat. He sets forth the character and work of the church in poetic figure, gives a dramatic presentation of her conflict with the state, speaks plainly of the abuses practiced by her representatives and by institutions within her pale, and holds up the great ideal which the church exists to realize. The most significant and most beautiful picture of the church is that embodied in " The Lady of the Lake " : [132]

> And near him stood the Lady of the Lake,
> Who knows a subtler magic than his own —
> Clothed in white samite, mystic, wonderful.
> She gave the king his huge cross-hilted sword,
> Whereby to drive the heathen out: a mist
> Of incense curl'd about her, and her face
> Well nigh was hidden in the minster gloom;
> But there was heard among the holy hymns,
> A voice as of the waters, for she dwells
> Down in a deep; calm, whatsoever storms
> May shake the world, and when the surface rolls,
> Has power to walk the waters like our Lord.[133]

Though her forms are ever changing, her great arms are outstretched with a constancy and might that cannot be broken. In " Gareth and Ly-

[132] " Coming of Arthur," p. 313.
[133] See also Stopford Brooke, *Tennyson: His Art and Relation to Modern Life*, pp. 260, 272.

nette," the poet says further of the Lady of
the Lake:

> All her dress
> Wept from her sides as water flowing away;
> But like the cross her great and goodly arms
> Stretch'd under all the cornice and upheld;
> And drops of water fell from either hand;
> And down from one a sword was hung, from one
> A censer, either worn with wind and storm;
> And o'er her breast floated the sacred fish;
> . . . . and over all,
> High on the top, were those three queens, the friends
> Of Arthur, who should help him at his need.[134]

The different parts of this picture have been thus
interpreted in their relation to the church:

The sword is the symbol of her justice, the censer
is the symbol of her adoration, and both bear the
marks of time and strife. The drops that fall from
her hands are the water of baptism, and the fish is the
ancient sign of the name of Christ. The three queens
who sit up aloft are the theological virtues of Faith,
Hope and Charity.[135]

The corruptions and abuses of the church are
portrayed with entire frankness and with dramatic
power. He speaks of the time

> when the monk was fat,
> And, issuing shorn and sleek,
> Would twist his girdle tight, and pat
> The girls upon the cheek.[136]

---

[134] P. 321.
[135] H. Van Dyke, *The Poetry of Tennyson*, pp. 173, 174.
[136] "The Talking Oak," p. 89.

Balin, after his encounter with Sir Garlon, entered the chapel of King Pellam, "in which he scarce could spy the Christ for Saints." [137] In "Sir John Oldcastle" these lines occur:

> The mitre-sanctioned harlot draws his clerks
> Into the suburb — their hard celibacy,
> Sworn to be veriest ice of pureness, molten
> Into adulterous living, or such crimes
> As holy Paul — a shame to speak of them
> Among the heathen —
> Sanctuary granted
> To bandit, thief, assassin — yea to him
> Who hacks his mother's throat — denied to him
> Who finds the Savior in his mother-tongue. [138]

In the same vein he continues:

> [I] rail'd at all the Popes, that ever since
> Sylvester shed the venom of world-wealth
> Into the church, had only prov'n themselves
> Poisoners, murderers. [139]

Columbus laments that in his great projects he was beaten back chiefly by the church, [140] to which he had always been true. [141] Cardinal Pole, in the drama of "Queen Mary," speaks thus of the English church:

[137] "Balin and Balan," p. 376.
[138] P. 523.
[139] P. 524.
[140] "Columbus," pp. 525, 526.
[141] P. 526.

> She seethed with such adulteries, and the lives
> Of many among your churchmen were so foul
> That heaven wept and earth blush'd.[142]

Cranmer inveighs

> Against the huge corruptions of the church,
> Monsters of mistradition.[143]

The dying King Edward says of priests and churches:

> Your Priests
> Gross, wordly, simoniacal, unlearned!
> They scarce can read their Psalter; and your churches
> Uncouth, unhandsome, while in Norman-land,
> God speaks thro' abler voices, as He dwells
> In statelier shrines.[144]

Becket declares:

> This Almoner hath tasted Henry's gold,
> The Cardinals have fingered Henry's gold,
> And Rome is venal ev'n to rottenness.[145]

Henry speaks of the "thread-bare-worn quarrel of Crown and Church." [146] Walter Map says, in graphic language: "If you boxed the Pope's ears with a purse, you might stagger him, but he would pocket the purse." [147] Robin

---

[142] Act III, sc. 4, p. 617.

[143] *Ibid.,* Act IV, sc. 2, p. 628.

[144] "Harold," Act I, sc. 1, p. 654.

[145] "Becket," Act I, sc. 3, p. 707.

[146] *Ibid.,* Act II, sc. 2, p. 719.

[147] *Ibid.,* p. 723.

speaks these words of condemnation to the
Friars:

> one of you
> Shamed a too trustful widow whom you heard
> In her confession; and another worse!
> An innocent maid.[148]

In a letter to his aunt, written in 1832, the poet
expresses his fear of the influence of the St.
Simonists in the church.

On the other hand, he has much to say of the
good wrought by the church as a whole, and by
individuals therein. He extends " To the Rev.
F. D. Maurice " a most hearty invitation to come
to his home, commending him as

> Being of that honest few,
> Who give the Fiend himself his due,
> Should eighty thousand College councils,
> Thunder Anathema, friend, at you.[149]

Says Becket:

> The people know their church a tower of strength,
> A bulwark against Throne and Baronage.[150]
> The Church is ever at variance with the kings,
> And ever at one with the poor.[151]

Perhaps as high commendation as the church
receives in any single sentence is that contained
in the emphatic utterance of the tyrant Henry:

[148] " The Foresters," Act III, sc. 1, p. 860.
[149] *Poems,* p. 234.
[150] " Becket," Act I, sc. 1, p. 699.
[151] *Ibid.,* sc. 4, p. 713.

"I would the church were down in hell." [152]
Such words from such a man can be considered
only as the highest eulogy. In the "Promise of
May" it was a Sister of Mercy, who had just
come from the deathbed of a pauper, who took
the unfortunate Eva to her home and cared for
her with tenderness and love. The outlaw Robin
recognized the poor priests as deserving to be
spared by his followers, "who spoiled the prior,
friar, abbot and monk." [153]

The pessimist in "Maud" declares that

The churchmen fain would kill their church,
As the churches have killed their Christ; [154]

but the poet believes that the church is being led
by the "hand that guides" to higher ideals and
greater achievements. In "In Memoriam" it is
the church bells upon which Tennyson calls to
"ring out the darkness of the land." It was
"upon the shrine" that Galahad saw the Holy
Grail descend.[155] The gleam,

Touch'd at the golden
Cross of the churches,

signifying that these are called to, "follow it,
follow the gleam." [156]

[152] *Ibid.,* Act V, sc. 1, p. 739.
[153] "The Foresters," Act III, sc. 1, p. 857.
[154] *Poems,* p. 305.
[155] "The Holy Grail," p. 426.
[156] "Merlin and the Gleam," pp. 830, 831.

Tennyson not only believed in the church as an institution; he believed specifically in the established church and openly opposed disestablishment. In a letter to Mr. Bosworth Smith, written in 1885, he says: " With you, I believe that the disestablishment and disendowment of the church, would prelude the downfall of much that is greatest and best in England. Abuses there are no doubt in the church, as elsewhere; but, these are not past remedy." [157] He was in hearty sympathy with such men as Maurice and Kingsley, who were striving to make thought more tolerant, and to impress upon all men the obligations of brotherhood. He favored changing " the spirit of the National Church by broadening its borders and deepening its spirituality," and he himself aided in bringing about this change.[158]

In these days of prolonged and earnest discussion concerning dogma and creed, it would be of interest to know just what Tennyson would have included in a statement of his own belief. But he steadily refused to formulate his creed, saying that people would not understand him if he did. If he had made the statement, we should have endeavored to understand him. As it is, we must be content with his own declaration

[157] *Review of Reviews,* December, 1892, p. 562.
[158] *Memoir,* Vol. I, p. 187.

that his poems express the principles at the foundation of his faith.[159] The goal to be sought is the union of thought with fact.[160] He hoped and believed that " the cramping creeds that had madden'd the people would vanish at last." [161] He honored men of the spirit of Akbar, who hated the rancor of castes and creeds, and wished to let men worship as they will.[162] He knew that all human creeds are " lower than the heart's desire." [163] " All the faiths of this grown world of ours " seemed to him to be too narrow.[164] He sympathized with those sincere souls who, in time of change and discovery and dispute,

Have hardly known what to believe, or whether,
They should believe in anything; the currents
So shift and change, they see not how they are borne,
Nor whither.[165]

He believed that Christ

wrought,
With human hands the creed of creeds,
In loveliness of perfect deeds.[166]

The nobility and beauty of a creed of deeds he

[159] *Ibid.,* pp. 308, 309.
[160] *Poems,* p. 65.
[161] " Despair," p. 545.
[162] " Akbar's Dream," p. 879.
[163] " Faith," p. 892.
[164] " Harold," Act III, sc. 2, p. 675.
[165] " Queen Mary," Act IV, sc. 3, p. 634.
[166] " In Memoriam," XXXVI, p. 257.

was always glad to portray. He did not accept every ancient religious tradition himself, and did not ask anyone else to do this. He declared:

> There lives more faith in honest doubt,
> Believe me, than in half the creeds.[167]

Such men as Maurice and Robertson believed that "In Memoriam" made a definite gain in the work of the reconciliation of religious philosophy with the progressive science of the day. They went farther than this and declared that he was the one poet who had really made an effective stand "on behalf of those first principles which underlie all creeds, which belong to our earliest childhood and on which the wisest and best have rested through all ages; that all is right; that darkness shall be clear; that God and Time are the only interpreters; that Love is King; that the Immortal is in us; that, which is the key-note of the whole, ' All is well, tho' Faith and Form be sundered in the night of fear.' " [168]

He believed in the freedom of the will with intensity of conviction. As a boy he happened upon the Calvinist creed. This led him to say: "However unfathomable the mystery, if one cannot believe in the freedom of the human will as of the Divine, life is hardly worth having." [169]

---

[167] *Ibid.*, XCVI, p. 274
[168] *Memoir*, Vol. I, p. 298.
[169] *Ibid.*, p. 317.

He recognized the promise in the work of Alexander Smith, but declared that he would have to learn a different creed from that in the line: " Fame, fame, thou are next to God." " Next to God," he repeated, " ' next to the Devil,' say I. Fame might be worth having, if it helped us to do good to a single mortal, but what is it? Only the pleasure of having one's self talked of up and down the street." [170]

He contended for " the larger faith " for all men; for the right of the individual to investigate and think for himself, without apology to his neighbor for the conclusions to which the truth led him. He looked forward to the time when Christianity without bigotry shall triumph, and when the controversies of creeds shall have vanished.[171] He believed that this result would be gained by living, not in external differences, but in fundamental unities. He agreed with Arthur Hallam " that the essential feelings of religion subsist in the utmost diversity of forms; " that " different language does not always imply different opinions, nor different opinions any difference in *real* faith." [172] He realized that every formal statement of truth must of necessity be imperfect, and therefore he had great sympathy

[170] *Ibid.*, p. 468.
[171] *Ibid.*, p. 326.
[172] *Ibid.*, p. 309.

with those who criticised such statements, pro-
vided they did not reject all spiritual truth in so
doing. His advice was: "Cling to faith beyond the forms of faith." At the same time, he
felt that definitions of truth have great importance and value for many people. He cau-
tioned the one who boasted that he was free
from bondage to formal faith, to beware lest, in
a world of so many confusions, he fail, "ev'n for
want of such a type." In the language of the
bishop of Ripon:

To him, as to so many, truth is so infinitely great that
all we can do with our poor human utterances is to
try and clothe it in such language as will make it clear
to ourselves, and clear to those to whom God sends
us with a message, but meanwhile, above us and our
thoughts — above our broken lights — God in his
mercy, God in his Love, God in his infinite nature is
greater than all.[173]

Tennyson's portraits of priests, friars, abbots,
monks, and clergymen are not such as to inspire
special confidence in the efficiency of the church
as a social institution, when it is remembered
how largely the work of the church is dependent
upon these official representatives. In the historical plays, and in poems portraying scenes and
events of historic interest, church officials and
the representatives of religious orders are pic-

[173] *Loc. cit.,* pp. 310, 311.

tured as they actually were. The truth does not flatter. But fact is better than flattery. It must be remembered that he is true to the time of which he is writing, and is not attempting to give his opinion of the church of today. Here are some lines which are typical of his treatment of degenerate church officials and monastic orders: " I am emptier than a friar's brains; " [174] " The poor man's money goes to fat the friar." [175] One of Wyatt's men in " Queen Mary " says: " I know not my letters; the old priests taught me nothing." [176] Becket says, in the drama bearing his name: " I cannot tell why monks should all be cowards." [177] Robin classes together " these proud priests, and these barons," as " devils that make this blessed England hell." [178] Priors, friars, abbots, monks, form an unholy group despised by Robin and his band,

> For playing upside down with Holy Writ,
> Sell all thou hast and give it to the poor;
> Take all they have and give it to thyself.[179]

There are other lines that picture clergymen of a type more familiar to the men of today,

[174] " Sir John Oldcastle," p. 521.
[175] *Ibid.*, p. 524.
[176] Act II, sc. 3, p. 601.
[177] Act V, sc. 2, p. 746.
[178] " The Foresters," Act III, sc. 1, p. 857.
[179] *Ibid.*

though scarcely more to be admired. Here is one:

> Half awake I heard,
> The parson taking wide and wider sweeps,
> Now harping on the church-commissioners,
> Now hawking at Geology and schism;
> Until I woke and found him settled down
> Upon the general decay of faith
> Right thro' the world, at home was little left,
> And none abroad; there was no anchor, none
> To hold by.[180]

The conclusion of this poem contains another reference to the same parson:

> At which the Parson, sent to sleep with sound,
> And waked with silence, grunted, " Good ! " but we
> Sat rapt.[181]

A man who could sleep through the reading of such a poem as " Morte D'Arthur " needs no other label to show the kind of a beast he is.

Someone has said that a man's estimate of woman is the measure of his manhood. The " fat-faced curate, Edward Bull," thus states his opinion of woman:

> I take it, God made the woman for the man
> And for the good and increase of the world.
> A pretty face is well, and this is well,
> To have a dame indoors, that trims us up
> And keeps us tight; but these unreal ways

[180] " The Epic," p. 67.
[181] P. 72.

Seem but the theme of writers, and indeed
Worn thread-bare.[182]

In " Sea Dreams " we have a picture of a clergyman of still another type:

A heated pulpiteer,
Not preaching simple Christ to simple men,
Announced the coming doom, and fulminated
Against the scarlet woman and her creed;
For sideways up he flung his arms, and shriek'd
" Thus, thus with violence," ev'n as if he held
The Apocalyptic mill stone, and himself
Were that great Angel; " Thus with violence
Shall Babylon be cast into the sea;
Then comes the close." [183]

In " Maud " we read of

The snowy-banded, dilettante,
Delicate handed priest, [184]

who intoned the service in the village church.
In " Despair " the man who attempted suicide
by drowning, and was saved by the minister of
the sect he had abandoned, thus addressed his
rescuer:

I know you of old —
Small pity for those that have ranged from the nar-
row warmth of your fold
Where you bawl'd the dark side of your faith, and a
God of eternal rage,

[182] " Edwin Morris," p. 83.
[183] P. 156.
[184] " Maud," VIII, p. 293.

'Till you flung us back on ourselves, and the human
heart and the Age.[185]

Becket calls Gilbert Foliot, bishop of London,
" A worldly follower of the worldly strong." [186]

The church warden, who has watched the methods by which clergymen have been promoted,
gives this wordly-wise advice to the curate. It
is significant as revealing the spirit of the church
of the time:

But Parson 'e will speak out, saw, now 'e be sixty-
seven,
He'll niver swap Owlby an' Scratby fur owt but the
kingdom o' Heaven;
An' thou'll be 'is Curate 'ere, but, if iver tha meäns to
git 'igher,
Tha mun tackle the sins o' the Wo'ld, an' not the faults
o' the Squire.
An' I reckons tha'll light of a livin' somewheers i' the
Wowd or the Fen,
If tha cottons down to thy betters, an' keeäps thysen to
thysen.
But niver not speäk plaäin out, if tha wants to git
forrards a bit,
But creeäp along the hedge-bottoms, an' thou'll be a
Bishop yit.[187]

Leigh Hunt, in a letter to S. C. Hall, has an
interesting comment upon the Tennysons which
sheds light upon this topic. The sarcasm is only

[185] *Poems,* p. 545.
[186] " Becket," Act I, sc. 3, p. 710.
[187] " The Church Warden and the Curate," p. 885.

the barb of the arrow of truth. He says:
" Charles is not equal to Alfred, but still partakes
of the genuine faculty. He has a graceful luxury, but combining less of the spiritual with it,
which I suppose is the reason why he has become
a clergyman." [188]

But there is another, and very different, type
of the clergyman given to us in the works of the
poet — a broader, abler, nobler, more self-sacrificing man, whose character reveals a higher mission for the church in human society. In the
" Conclusion " of " The May Queen " we have a
reference to this higher type of minister:

But still I think it can't be long before I find release;
And that good man, the clergyman, has told me words
    of peace,
O blessings on his kindly voice and on his silver hair!
And blessings on his whole life long, until he meet me
    there!
O blessings on his kindly heart and on his silver head!
A thousand times I blest him, as he knelt beside my
    bed.[189]

The lines " To J. M. K." portray a clergyman
as admirable, but of the more military type:

My hope and heart is with thee — thou wilt be
A latter Luther, and a soldier priest
To scare church-harpies from the Master's feast;
Our dusted velvets have much need of thee;

[188] *Memoir,* Vol. I, p. 164.
[189] P. 52.

Thou art no sabbath-drawler of old saws,
Distill'd from some worm-canker'd homily,
But spurr'd at heart with fieriest energy,
To embattail and to wall about thy cause
With iron-worded proof, hating to hark
The humming of the drowsy pulpit-drone
Half God's good sabbath, while the wornout clerk
Brow-beats his desk below. Thou from a throne
Mounted in heaven will shoot into the dark
Arrows of lightnings. I will stand and mark.[190]

Cranmer in his time of peril asked pity, not for himself, but for " the poor flock," the women and the children who held with him.[191] Becket fed the poor and was loved by the people.[192] Up to the very last Becket defended his flock, though ready to die himself.

Tennyson showed by his friendships the type of minister which he most honored. One of his old and highly esteemed college friends was Mr. Rashdall, the clergyman of Malvern. This man was deeply loved by his parishioners, and was so simple and direct in his preaching that he had emptied the Dissenting chapels for miles around. He often held his church services in the fields.[193] Maurice was also an intimate friend of the poet, and was honored as an able, courageous, and thor-

---

[190] P. 25.
[191] " Queen Mary," Act IV, sc. 2, p. 629.
[192] " Becket," Act I, sc. 4, p. 714; also Act V, sc. 2, p. 741.
[193] Memoir, Vol. I, p. 355.

oughly honest minister of the church. Tennyson considered him the foremost thinker among the churchmen of the time, though [194] the sermons of Robertson, of Brighton, seemed to him the most spiritual utterances coming from any minister of his day. It is such men as these that make the church a social institution of real importance in the progress of the world.

[194] *Ibid.,* p. 430.

CHAPTER VIII

DEMOCRACY AND PROGRESS

By a democracy we understand a government in which the supreme power is directly exercised or controlled by the people collectively. A democracy in name is not necessarily one in fact. A government called by some other name may be a democracy in reality. What Tennyson says in regard to the people as a class is of interest to us as indicating his views of the policy of putting supreme governmental power in their hands. There are some lines that would give us reason to infer that the poet had not great confidence in the wisdom, the ability, or the character of the masses. St. Simeon Stylites calls the people who take him for a saint " silly " and " foolish." [1] In " The Vision of Sin " these lines occur:

> Welcome, fellow-citizens,
> Hollow hearts and empty heads.[2]

When Merlin the Wise compares the harlot to the crowd, he gives his judgment of the people as well as of the scarlet woman:

[1] " St. Simeon Stylites," pp. 87, 88.
[2] P. 122.

And in this
Are harlots like the crowd, that if they find
Some stain or blemish in a name of note,
Not grieving that their greatest are so small,
Inflate themselves, with some insane delight,
And judge all Nature from her feet of clay,
Without the will to lift their eyes, and see
Her Godlike head crown'd with spiritual fire
And touching other worlds.   I am weary of her.[3]

Tiresias does not express any higher opinion
of the wisdom of the people.   He says:

When the crowd would roar
For blood, for war, whose issue was their doom,
To cast wise words among the multitude
Was flinging fruit to lions.

. . . .

I would that I were gathered to my rest
And mingled with the famous kings of old,
On whom about their ocean-islets flash
The faces of the Gods — the wise man's word,
Here trampled by the populace underfoot,
There crown'd with worship.[4]

The same estimate, coupled with a strong statement of the untruthfulness of the multitude is
given in " Vastness " :

Lies upon this side, lies upon that side, truthless violence mourn'd by the wise,
Thousands of voices drowning his own in a popular
torrent of lies.[5]

[3] " Merlin and Vivien," p. 393.
[4] " Tiresias," pp. 539, 540.
[5] P. 812.

The common people have from the remotest times been bearers of burdens, victims of tyranny and oppression. This truth of history the poet has not failed to portray. This is the representation in " The Palace of Art ":

The people here, a beast of burden slow,
Toil'd onward, prick'd with goads and stings.[6]

In " Locksley Hall " he used a figure he gained from reading Pringle's *Travels,* to indicate the slow advance of a suffering people:

Slowly comes a hungry people, as a lion creeping nigher,
Glares at one that nods and winks behind a slowly-dying fire.[7]

Godiva knew of the burdens of the people and " loathed to see them overtaxed."

But whatever may be the theory concerning the right of the people to exercise power in government, that power has actually been exercised in the past to a greater or less extent. To the poet the signs indicate an increase rather than a diminution of it in the future. The speaker in " Locksley Hall " sees " the standards of the people plunging thro' the thunder storm." [8] This observation of the tendency of the time finds ex-

[6] P. 46.
[7] P. 101.
[8] P. 101.

pression even in " In Memoriam." One asks the mourner :

> Is this an hour
> For private sorrow's barren song,
> When more and more the people throng
> The chairs and thrones of civil power ? [9]

The devoted Edith asserts that Harold is not to be the last English king of England, but

> First of a line coming from the people,
> And chosen by the people. [10]

Antonius speaks a good word for the common throng, when he says to the lustful Synorix :

> I have heard them say in Rome,
> That your own people cast you from their bounds,
> For some unprincely violence to a woman,
> As Rome did Tarquin. [11]

It is undoubtedly true, as has been stated by a careful student of English social and political life, that many of the " equality " ideas current in England came from France. It may not be exactly agreeable to an Englishman to admit the correctness of this statement, but any unprejudiced observer familiar with the social history of both countries will find no good reason seriously to question it. The hopes that the

[9] XXI, p. 253.
[10] " Harold," Act V, sc. 1, p. 687.
[11] " The Cup," Act I, sc. 1, p. 751.

French patriots, with their motto of "liberty,
equality, and fraternity," aroused in the minds of
men were crushed to earth by the horrors of the
Revolution. But the principles at the foundation of that great struggle were thus brought to
the attention of the world, and have never since
been forgotten. They became effective in two
ways: first, by securing the enthusiastic support
of those who came to believe in them when
definitely stated; and, second, by arousing the
determined opposition of the conservatives who
believed that such principles are pernicious and
tend to the overthrow of established government.
The French struggle for liberty clarified the ideas
of the world by setting out in bold relief the principles for which the struggle stood, and calling
for a division of the house.

"Equality" is a word which has been greatly
misunderstood. If it meant that every man has
the same intellectual and moral power as every
other man, and should have the same political
and financial possessions, it is an absurdity that
needs only to be stated to be recognized. Yet
this is what many foreigners supposed the
"equality" cry of France to signify. If understood to mean equality of opportunity, it would
win more adherents and arouse less violent opposition. Tennyson does not dwell upon this
theme. His references to it make it evident that

he shared the common dread of the proclamation of doctrines that had brought commotion, anarchy, and bloodshed into Paris. In " Aylmer's Field " he speaks of " that cursed France with her egalities." [12]   He has no confidence in the sanity of the " passionate shriek for the rights of an equal humanity " that had echoed again and again in the streets of Paris.[13]   It was the Princess, whose views of human society were greatly altered by her experiment with her college, who said :

All things serve their time
Toward that great year of equal mights and rights.[14]

Tennyson, when speaking for himself, would have described the millennial year in different terms.   His own contempt for the false idea of equality, in which many people trusted, is expressed perhaps best of all in " Locksley Hall Sixty Years After " :

Envy wears the mask of Love, and laughing sober fact to scorn,
Cries to Weakest as to Strongest, Ye are equals, equal born !
Equal-born? O yes, if yonder hill be level with the flat.
Charm us, Orator, till the Lion look no larger than the Cat,

[12] P. 146.
[13] " Beautiful City," p. 835.
[14] " The Princess," p. 187.

Till the Cat thro' that mirage of overheated language
    loom,
Larger than the Lion — Demos end in working its own
    doom.[15]

Tennyson dreaded, feared the control of the
ignorant, passionate crowd. He believed that
the masses could be captured by demagogues with
crude theories and wild schemes. He exhorts
the patriot not to

    Feed with crude imaginings
    The herd, wild hearts and feeble wings
    That every sophister can lime.[16]

He did not want in England the " brainless mobs
and lawless Powers " of France.[17] These meant
to him only " brute control," [18] and he believed
that " the tyranny of all leads backward to the
tyranny of one." [19] The freedom England had
gained might be lost " thro' the tonguesters." [20]
He adds ironically:

You that woo the voices — tell them " old experience is
    a fool "
Teach your flatter'd kings that only those who cannot
    read can rule.[21]

[15] P. 563.
[16] P. 65.
[17] " Wellington Ode," p. 219.
[18] *Ibid.*, p. 220.
[19] " Tiresias," p. 539.
[20] " Locksley Hall Sixty Years After," p. 564.
[21] *Ibid.*

If the masses come into power, they cannot be relied upon; for "the many will feel no shame to give themselves the lie." [22]   He was too ardent a lover of liberty to tolerate with any composure "that tyranny of a majority in which alone a material omnipotence is united with a legal one." [23]

Yet, despite such lines as these that have been quoted, Tennyson was a believer in the true democracy, the Greek idea of which is "the public good."   Mr. Sydney Webb affirms that in America democracy means "equality," while in England it means government of the people, by the people, and for the people.   If this distinction be a real one, it would be entirely correct to say that the poet believed in the English, but not in the American, type of democracy.   There can be no doubt of his willingness to give his cordial support to the English system.   The historical plays contain frequent reference to the fact that England's rulers are the actual choice of her people, and her laws the expression of the people's will.   He conceived it to be the duty of the crown and the statesman to see that such conditions are maintained, and that from time to time such changes are made as are demanded by new needs and new ideas.   Whether democracy in America

[22] "The Cup," Act II, p. 761.
[23] *Memoir*, Vol. I, p. 506.

means equality may be a serious question. Those who see it at short range are more inclined to the opinion that it means the tyranny of the "machine" and the "boss"; but this is, of course, a perversion of the early and true ideal of the republic. Tennyson expressed a sincere admiration for the constitution of the United States. Writing to Walt Whitman in 1887, he said: "Truly the Mother Country . . . . may feel that how much-soever the daughter owes to her, she, the mother, has nevertheless something to learn from the daughter. Especially I would note the care taken to guard a noble constitution from rash and unwise innovations." [24] In a letter to Mr. Bosworth Smith, written two years earlier, he says: "As to any vital changes in our constitution, I could wish that some of our prominent politicians who look to America as their ideal might borrow from her an equivalent to that conservatively restrictive provision under the fifth article of her Constitution. I believe that it would be a great safeguard to our own in these days of ignorant and reckless theorists." [25] He had confidence that the throne of the queen of whom he wrote would be "unshaken still,"

[24] *Review of Reviews,* December, 1892, p. 562.
[25] *Loc. cit.*

because it was " broad-based upon her people's will." [26]

With all the perils of the time, with all the demagoguery and cries of revolution, Tennyson still believed in the " common sense of most " that would " hold a fretful realm in awe." [27] The great problems may have to look to the future for their complete solution, but there will come a time when " crowds at length will be sane." [28] This " crown'd Republic's crowning common sense " has " saved her many times," [29] and there is reason to believe that this good sense is in increasing rather than diminishing. There are still

> Men loud against all forms of power —
> Unfurnish'd brows, tempestuous tongues —
> Expecting all things in an hour —
> Brass mouths and iron lungs;

but there is still the vision

> Of Knowledge fusing class with class,
> Of civic Hate no more to be,
> Of Love to leaven all the mass,
> Till every soul be free.[30]

[26] " To the Queen," p. 1.
[27] " Locksley Hall," p. 101.
[28] " Wellington Ode," p. 220.
[29] " To the Queen," p. 475.
[30] " Freedom," p. 576.

The social conditions desired by the wise cannot be brought about in an hour. Political power is coming more and more into the possession of the people, but this power must not be placed in the hands of the ignorant and the passionate. Those who are to bear responsibilities must be trained to bear them well, for the " public good " according to the old Greek idea. There must be some sort of " universal culture for the crowd." [31]

Tennyson's interest in the poor and humble gives to many of his poems, and those among the best he ever wrote, a genuinely democratic flavor. He was always in sympathy with the cause of liberal reform. His only vote in the House of Lords was given in favor of the enfranchisement of the agricultural laborer; [32] but this was because he believed that the agricultural laborer was prepared for the ballot. He said that the two great social questions impending in England were " the housing and education of the poor man before making him our master, and the higher education of women." [33] Those who were prepared to serve the public weal he wanted to see sharers in the government; but no one should be asked or permitted to bear such responsibilities who was unfit to bear them for the good of all. This was

[31] " The Princess," p. 167.
[32] *Review of Reviews,* December, 1892, p. 562.
[33] *Memoir,* Vol. I, p. 249.

to him a fundamental principle of the true democracy for which he stood and which he preached to others. Thus, ruler and people could work together for the highest ends —" one for all and all for one, one soul." [34]

It is evident, from words already quoted, that Tennyson considered the two great social questions in England largely questions of education. The great need of educaton among the poor, and especially among women, is shown often in the poems, though he does not lose sight of the general truth implied in the words of Balin, as he looked upon Lancelot:

> These be gifts,
> Born with the blood, not learnable, divine,
> Beyond my reach.[35]

The contemptuous comments of " The Village Wife " upon the actions of the Squire who wrote a " book himself," and gave a big price for " an owd scatted stoän," and prized a brown pot and a bone which he dug out of the earth, and bought old coins that could not be passed with the queen's gold, and " bowt little statutes all-naäkt an' which was a shaäme to be seen," and " niver knowd nowt but booöks, an' booöks, as thou knaws, beänt nowt; " such comments as these reveal intellectual needs that are appealing as well

---

[34] " Harold," Act II, sc. 3, p. 681.
[35] " Balin and Balan," p. 372.

as ludicrous. In the household of the squire " the lasses " tore the leaves out of the middle of valuable books to kindle the fire.[36] One of Wyatt's men declared that he didn't know his letters, " because the old priests had taught him nothing." [37] Farmer Steer admitted that he had no time to make himself " a scholard " while he was making himself a gentleman. Allen, the farm laborer, says that he " were born afoor schoolintime." [38]

Attempts have always been made to meet in some way such needs as these. The methods employed did not always commend themselves to the judgment of the poet. His criticisms upon educators, upon schools, upon the studies pursued and the methods of teaching, enable us to judge of the educational ideal which seemed to him most worthy of being cherished. In " The Princess " one

> Discussed his tutor, rough to common men,
> But honeying at the whisper of a lord;
> And one the Master as a rogue in grain
> Veneer'd with sanctimonious theory.[39]

These species are not extinct, and Tennyson had for them the same contempt which every true man has today. In the same poem we have at

[36] P. 515.
[37] " Queen Mary," Act II, sc. 3, p. 601.
[38] " The Promise of May," Act I, p. 782; Act III, p. 795.
[39] P. 167.

least a partial description of the course of study in the "University for maidens." Here is a narrative of a half-day spent in "stately theatres bench'd crescent-wise":

> in each we sat, we heard,
> The grave Professor. On the lecture slate
> The *circle* rounded under female hands
> With flawless demonstration; followed then
> A *classic* lecture rich in sentiment,
> With scraps of thundrous *Epic* lilted out
> By violet hooded Doctors, elegies
> And quoted odes and jewels five words long
> That on the stretch'd fore-finger of all Time
> Sparkle for ever; then we dipt in all
> That treats of whatsoever is, the state,
> The total chronicles of man, the mind,
> The morals, something of the frame, the rock,
> The star, the bird, the fish, the shell, the flower,
> Electric chemic laws, and all the rest,
> And whatsoever can be taught and known.[40]

Tennyson revisited Cambridge, where he and Arthur Hallam had been companions, and went to the room "where," he says,

> Once we held debate, a band
> Of youthful friends, on mind and art
> And labour and the changing mart,
> And all the frame work of the land.[41]

In a letter to his aunt, written early in his college days, he does not speak with great enthu-

[40] *Ibid.*, pp. 178, 179.
[41] "In Memoriam," LXXXVII, p. 270.

siasm of his university life. He says: "I know
not how it is, but I feel isolated here, in the
midst of society. The country is so disgustingly
level, the revelry of the place so monotonous, the
studies of the University so uninteresting, so
much matter of fact. None but dry-headed, calculating, angular little gentlemen can take much
delight in them." [42] This was his candid opinion
of the conditions prevailing in the Cambridge
of his day. The course of study seemed to him
narrow and dry. He was impatient with the
lethargy there, with the lack of any "teaching
that grappled with the ideas of the age, and
stimulated and guided thought on the subjects
of deepest human interest." These lines, descriptive of the Cambridge of 1830, have been published in the *Memoir* by his son:

Therefore, your Halls, your ancient Colleges,
Your portals statued with old kings and queens,
Your gardens, myriad-volumed libraries,
Wax-lighted chapels, and rich carven screens,
Your doctors, and your proctors, and your deans,
Shall not avail you, when the Day beam sports,
New risen o'er awaken'd Albion. No!
Nor yet your solemn organ pipes that blow
Melodious thunders thro' your vacant courts
At noon and eve, because your manner sorts
Not with this age wherefrom ye stand apart,
Because the lips of little children preach

[42] *Memoir,* Vol. I, p. 34.

Against you, you that do profess to teach
And teach us nothing, feeding not the heart.[43]

Cambridge changed with the years, and he afterward regretted such bitter words as these. When the university adapted itself to modern requirements, he honored it as much as before he had condemned it.   He went back to Cambridge in 1872.   What impressed him most at that time was the change for the better in the relations between don and undergraduate. Speaking to Dr. Butler of the time when he was a student at the great university (1828–31), he said: "There was a want of love in Cambridge then."   In 1872, however, he found teacher and student on terms of personal friendship and ever ready for an interchange of ideas.   This change he believed would have the most helpful influence on the opinions, sympathies, and aspirations of generations to come.   In this view he is entirely at one with some of the comparatively recent utterances of prominent educators in America. The change has begun to be made in some of the great educational institutions of this land.   It is one of the hopeful signs, and the cloud of promise is already larger than a man's hand.

The institutions for the higher education of women should say to those to be benefited by

[43] *Ibid.*, pp. 66, 67.

their opportunities what the Princess said to her maidens:

> Work out your freedom, Girls,
> Knowledge is now no more a fountain seal'd.[44]

The various characters in the poem give many different views upon the higher education of women. In the end, the Princess, whom Tennyson considered one of the noblest among his women, comes to a sane and sensible conclusion, and recognizes the relation she holds to her Creator and to society.

The ironical lines in "Locksley Hall Sixty Years After,"

> Feed the budding rose of boyhood, with the drainage of your sewer:
>
> . . . .
>
> Set the maiden fancies wallowing in the troughs of Zolaism,

express the poet's detestation of the impure in literature and life, and his fear of its influence upon the young.[45] By his words and example, Tennyson urged men to banish such influences by the substitution of those of opposite character. His own school days at Louth were not happy. He was at the mercy of "a tempestuous, flogging master of the old stamp," and was brutally cuffed by a big lad because he was a new boy. In later

[44] "The Princess," p. 174.
[45] P. 564.

years he said: "How I did hate that school! The only good I ever got from it was the memory of the words 'sonus desilientis aquae' and of an old wall covered with wild weeds opposite the school window." [46]   Professor Hale gives an interesting account of Louth School, and the reader of it cannot wonder at Tennyson's hatred of this Educational Gehenna.[47]

Tennyson was devoted to his own children, and made them his companions after the most civilized and Christian ideals of modern times. He raced with them up hill and down dale, read to them, played football or built castles with them, and taught them to shoot with bow and arrow, or went flower-hunting with them. If it was stormy, he would build cities of brick for the children, play battledore and shuttlecock, blow bubbles with them, help them to act charades or scenes from some well-known play. In the autumn he would work with them, brushing up leaves, making new glades through the shrubs, or reshingling old paths. His chief anxiety was that his children should be truthful. He impressed this lesson upon them so that they never forgot it. Children thus trained in the home certainly ought to be well prepared to take their

[46] *Memoir*, Vol. I, pp. 6, 7.
[47] *Ibid.*, p. 497, Appendix.

places as intelligent, working members of human society.

Unfortunately, all children are not thus prepared for their work in the world, and this deficiency in education must be made good in later years, so far as possible, if the highest interests of society are to be subserved. To meet this need, in part at least, the university-extension movement was called into existence. Tennyson early appreciated the importance of this work and gave to it his hearty approval. He believed that there was very great social significance in so practical a plan devised to give to those outside the favored classes the advantages of the higher education and culture. Upon it he built large hopes for the future of the people.[48]

When the Chartist and socialist agitations assumed alarming intensity and proportions, many advocated imprisonment and violent repression for their participants. The poet discountenanced all such threatened punitive measures, and urged instead a more widespread national education, as the real remedy for social disorders. He hoped especially that the Bible would be read and studied by all classes of people, and expounded simply by their teachers. He declared that " the Bible ought to be read, were it only for the sake of the grand English in which it is written, an

[48] *Memoir,* Vol. I, p. 68.

education in itself." [49]   At the same time, he believed that the education of every boy should prepare him to defend his country in time of national peril.   To Colonel Richards, who was
prominent in the formation of vounteer rifle corps
in 1859, he wrote: " I hope that you will not
cease from your labors until it is the law of the
land that every male child in it shall be trained
to the use of arms." [50]   This was in his judgment
the best way to maintain peace.   He believed
that every child should be trained to save the
state in time of danger, as well as to minister to
its highest progress in time of peace.   An education which does not reach all of the people, to
develop the resources of individuals, and educate
them for their places in the social body, was to
him a defective system.   He desired a democracy
made up of persons whose powers are developed
by education, and who are trained to serve their
fellow-men and the state by the arts of peace,
and to defend the nation in time of war.   A
democracy of demagoguery and artificial equality
was to him a menace and an abhorrence.

True education does not consist merely in acquiring or imparting knowledge.   It is bringing
all the powers of the individual to normal development for their work in the world.   The

[49] *Ibid.*, p. 308.
[50] *Ibid.*, p. 436.

progress of the individual and of the race is,
however, largely impeded by ignorance. Therefore knowledge has a distinct social mission to
fulfil. A part of the work of him who loves his
land is to " make knowledge circle with the
winds." [51]   Doing this, he may be

> Certain, if knowledge bring the sword,
> That knowledge takes the sword away.[52]

This principle is illustrated by the schoolboy who
is cruel " ere he grow to pity — more from ignorance than will." [53]   When his ignorance is banished, his cruelty is done away. Wherever in
life that which knows not rules that which knows,
it is to its own harm.[54]   All classes need knowledge. When they gain it, they will be fused into
one great brotherhood; for it is ignorance that
divides class from class.[55]

Knowledge can certainly do much for the
world. It not only does away with the tyranny
of ignorance and fuses class with class; it does
much to make men free.[56]   Yet at present it is
very imperfect. A thousand things are hidden

[51] "Love Thou Thy Land," p. 65.
[52] P. 66.
[53] "Walking to the Mail," p. 82.
[54] "To the Queen," p. 475.
[55] "Freedom," p. 576.
[56] "The Princess," p. 202.

for a hundred that are known.[57]   One of the
grave dangers of the time is a too great depend-
ence upon knowledge.   There is much that it
cannot do.   It is at best only one of three forces
that must always work together:

> Beauty, Good and Knowledge are three sisters,
> That never can be sundered without tears.[58]

It is a great mistake to suppose that knowledge is
" all in all." [59]   Of one who held to that opinion
it is written:

> Something wild within her breast,
> A greater than all knowledge beat her down.[60]

Knowledge may claim too high a rank:

> Let her know her place;
>   She is second, not the first.[61]

Vivien the harlot conquered Merlin the sage.[62]
" The Ancient Sage " declares,

> Knowledge is the swallow on the lake,
> That sees and stirs the surface-shadow there
> But never yet hath dipt into the abysm.[63]

[57] " Mechanophilus," p. 890.
[58] *Memoir,* Vol. I, p. 119.
[59] " The Princess," p. 171.
[60] *Ibid.,* p. 213.
[61] " In Memoriam," CXIV, p. 280.
[62] " Merlin and Vivien," p. 395.
[63] *Poems,* p. 548.

This is the partial and imperfect knowledge that we possess.

> It leads to something higher and better,
> Utter knowledge is but utter love.[64]

As it points to that which is higher and leads the way, it fulfils its most exalted mission. This is the estimate put upon knowledge in the education of the individual and the race by one whom Thackeray pronounced the wisest man he knew.[65]

Science is one of the special departments of knowledge in which Tennyson was most deeply interested. He gloried in its achievements, and at the same time recognized its limitations. The surgeon in " The Children's Hospital " " was happier using the knife than in trying to save the limb," [66] and was heard to mutter: " The good Lord Jesus has had his day." [67] In " Queen Mary " he refers to the time when the " letting of the blood " was a common method of treatment employed by physicians.[68] He does not regard science as infallible, as do many who delight in juggling with pretentious terms. He reserves the right to refuse to accept the dicta of science, if in his judgment they are not true. He says:

[64] " The Ring," p. 814.
[65] *Memoir*, Vol. I, p. 419.
[66] " In the Children's Hospital," p. 517.
[67] *Ibid.*
[68] Act III, sc. 2, p. 609.

> Not only cunning casts in clay
> Let science prove we are, and then
> What matters Science unto men,
> At least to me?   I would not stay.[69]

Akbar, quoting the hymn to heaven, sings:

> All the tracks
> Of Science making toward thy perfectness
> Are blinding desert sand; we scarce can spell
> The Alif of Thine Alphabet of Love.[70]

Yet true science has lofty ideals which it is constantly approaching.   Now we are at a time

> When Science reaches forth her arms
> To feel from world to world, and charms
> Her secret from the latest moon?[71]

There is no real ground for discouragement in the fact that " science moves but slowly, slowly, creeping on from point to point." [72]   The progress made by science has been real progress.   In the year of the queen's jubilee, 1887, he and the English people could look back upon " fifty years of ever-brightening Science." [73]

These lines in the poems are passing glimpses of the life of Tennyson himself.   He counted among his most valued friends such eminent

[69] " In Memoriam," CXX, p. 281.
[70] " Akbar's Dream," p. 879.
[71] " In Memoriam," XXI, p. 253.
[72] " Locksley Hall," p. 101.
[73] *Poems,* p. 805.

scientists as the Duke of Argyll,[74] Lord Lilford, the well-known ornithologist,[75] and Professor Tyndall.[76] He showed great interest in the scientific discoveries of his time.[77] He read Darwin's *Origin of Species* [78] and Herschel's *Astronomy,*[79] studied geology at Farringford with the local geologist, and continually used the platform on the top of his house to observe the stars.[80] Moreover, he was careful, painstaking, and successful in his scientific study. Some years before the publication of " Vestiges of Creation," in 1844, the sections of " In Memoriam " about evolution had been read to his friends. Of natural selection Romanes said: " In ' In Memoriam ' Tennyson noted the fact, and a few years later Darwin supplied the explanation." [81] The way in which eminent scientific men looked upon the poet is indicated by the biographer who says that " scientific leaders like Herschel, Owen, Sedgwick, and Tyndall regarded him as a champion of Science and cheered him with words of genuine admiration for his love of Nature, for

[74] *Memoir*, Vol. I, p. 339.
[75] *Ibid.*, p. 414.
[76] *Ibid.*, p. 427.
[77] *Ibid.*, p. 185.
[78] *Ibid.*, p. 443.
[79] *Ibid.*, p. 356.
[80] *Ibid.*, p. 431.
[81] *Ibid.*, p. 223.

the eagerness with which he welcomed all the latest scientific discoveries, and for his trust in truth.   Science indeed in his opinion was one of the main forces tending to disperse the superstition that still darkens the world." [82]   They also strongly commended his scientific references as being true to the facts.   One of the most famous physicians for the insane said of the mad-scene in " Maud " that it was " the most faithful representation of madness since Shakespeare." [83] " Maud " is not a treatise on insanity, nor is any poem of Tennyson's an essay on botany or ornithology.   Rev. B. Jowett, in a letter to Mrs. Tennyson, gives a sensible word upon the subject. He says: " Have not many sciences such as Astronomy or Geology a side of feeling which is poetry?   No sight touches ordinary persons so much as a starlight night." [84]

Tennyson's positive acceptance of the doctrine of evolution undoubtedly did much to win for him the cordial approval of scientific men.   His belief in the truth of this hypothesis of science influenced largely his doctrine of the individual and of society.   Evolution may not make a man proud of the past, but it gives him a most wonderful hope for the future and counsels patience

[82] *Ibid.,* pp. 298, 299.
[83] *Ibid.,* p. 398.
[84] *Ibid.,* p. 433.

with the present. Someone has said that, " if
man was once an ape, there is all the greater
reason to believe that he will one day be an
angel." One can cheerfully labor and suffer if he
is confident that in the end the product will justify
the process. As far back as the years spent in
Cambridge, Tennyson propounded the remarkable theory that the " development of the human
body might possibly be traced from the radiated,
vermicular, moluscous, and vertebrate organ-
isms." Whatever may have been the significance
of that statement made by him in a college discussion, when the theory of organic evolution
was seriously suggested by science, Tennyson
was prepared to accept it. It came into his
poetry because it was a part of himself. " So
many a million of ages have gone to the making
of man," [85] and so great progress has already
been made that it inspires the hope that in the
ages to come he will become " no longer half
akin to brute." [86]

In " The Promise of May " Edgar speaks of
man as " the child of Evolution." [87] In the
Memoir two or three stanzas are quoted that are
of special interest as bearing upon this theme.

[85] " Maud," p. 290.
[86] " In Memoriam," p. 286.
[87] Act I, p. 784.

After the old verse XXVI of the "Palace of
Art" were these lines:

> From shape to shape at first within the womb,
>   The brain is molded, she began,
> And thro' all phases of all thought I come
>   Unto the perfect man.
> All nature widens upward. Evermore
>   The simpler essence lower lies,
> More complex is more perfect, owning more
>   Discourse, more widely wise.[87a]

Mr. Herbert Spencer was particularly interested
in "The Two Voices," and in a letter to the poet
quoted the lines:

> Or if thro' lower lives I came —
> Thro' all experience past became
> Consolidate in mind and frame.

With the letter he sent a copy of his *Psychology*,
which he said, " applies to the elucidation of mental science, the hypothesis to which you refer." [88]
    Tennyson faced with boldness the objections
urged against the theory. He knew that the
single life is ruthlessly sacrificed, that " a
thousand types are gone." [89]   He held firmly to
the belief in the freedom of the will. He recognized the possibility of degeneration as well as
of progress. He saw

[87a] *Memoir,* Vol. I, pp. 119, 120.
[88] *Ibid.,* p. 411.
[89] " In Memoriam," LV, LVI, p. 261.

> Evolution ever climbing after some ideal good
> And reversion ever dragging Evolution in the mud.[90]

But his hope was still large for the future. He declared: "We are far from the noon of man, there is time for the race to grow." [91] The race is growing, and man is being made. The whole record of the past indicates that we are moving toward the light. Man is being trained to take his share in the work of the world. This makes true democracy a certainty of the future, and a promised blessing, not a menace. To demand and force in a democracy that for which men are not prepared is revolution, and retards instead of hastens the progress of the race. To-day many things are to us mysterious, because

> the goal of this great world
> Lies beyond sight.[92]

Tennyson loved to live in the future. He called that his "world." [93] He said: "To me often the far-off world seems nearer than the present, for in the present is always something unreal and indistinct, but the other seems a good solid planet, rolling round its green hills and

[90] "Locksley Hall Sixty Years After," p. 565.
[91] "The Dawn," p. 889.
[92] "To the Queen," p. 475.
[93] *Memoir,* Vol. I, p. 168.

paradises to the harmony of more steadfast laws." [94]   It was Merlin the Wise who said:

> my blood,
> Hath earnest in it of far springs to be, [95]

and that inner prophecy of a grander future for the individual and the world the poet felt in himself.   What the coming days have in store for us no mortal man can fully or accurately describe. We are sure that

> Far away beyond her myriad coming changes earth will be
> Something other than the wildest modern guess of you and me. [96]

There are new developments awaiting us in the future.   Of that we are confident, though we cannot describe them in detail.   Our sons will surpass us as we have exceeded the achievements of our fathers. [97]   The Light will be Victor. [98]

> England, France, all man to be,
> Will make one people ere man's race be run. [99]

The future, truthfully conceived, solves many of the riddles of the present.   Of the mysteries he says:

[94] *Ibid.*, pp. 171, 172.
[95] " Merlin and Vivien," p. 389.
[96] " Locksley Hall Sixty Years After," p. 566.
[97] " Mechanophilus," p. 890.
[98] " On the Jubilee of Queen Victoria," p. 806.
[99] " To Victor Hugo," p. 534.

> Our playwright may show
> In some fifth Act what this wild drama means.[100]

There is much hopeless pessimism in the world, and this fact of life finds abundant expression in the poetry of Tennyson. The man who suffers and loses may despair of himself. The man who observes and thinks may become hopeless concerning the possibilities of human nature. The one who reflects upon the history of peoples may despair of the future progress of the race. All these phases of pessimism are faithfully pictured in the poems. In " The Two Voices " one says to him:

> Thou art so steep'd in misery,
> Surely 'twere better not to be.[101]

In " The Promise of May," Harold exclaims:

> Better death with our first wail than life.[102]

In " Vastness " one asks the question:

> What is it all, if we all of us end but in being our own
>   corpse-coffins at last,
> Swallow'd in Vastness, lost in Silence, drown'd in the
>   deeps of a meaningless Past? [103]

The same spirit is revealed in " Locksley Hall." Many lines in " Maud " are expressive of the

[100] " The Play," p. 836.
[101] P. 31.
[102] Act II, p. 790.
[103] P. 813.

same pessimism that is blind to everything except the lower and grosser facts of the material
world.   One will serve as a type of all :   " Cheat
and be cheated and die; who knows?   We are
ashes and dust." [104]

Harold discarded the philosophy that teaches
that the mind of the child is a " tabula rasa," and
exclaimed :

> There, there is written in invisible inks
> " Lust, Prodigality, Covetousness, Craft,
> Cowardice, Murder "— and the heat and fire
> Of life will bring them out, and black enough,
> So the child grow to manhood.[105]

In " Geraint and Enid " the despair of the individual and of human nature is also affirmed of
the race.   It is the logical inference.   " O pur-
blind race of miserable men " is the statement
of this conclusion.[106]   It is essentially the same
thought that is embodied in such lines as this in
" Maud ":   " Wretchedest age, since Time began." [107]   The young man who is the chief
speaker in this poem sees evil glaring out from
all social arrangements.   He sees despicable
meanness and selfishness in every human form.
Becoming discontented and cynical, his utter-

[104] P. 287.
[105] " The Promise of May," Act II, pp. 789, 790.
[106] P. 354.
[107] V, II, p. 305.

ances are the expression of the typical pessimism
of his day.

While this phase of thought is truthfully portrayed by the poet because it is a part of life,
there can be no doubt that Tennyson himself was
a consistent optimist. He had his moods of de-
pression and despondency and despair, and these
it is not difficult to trace in his writings; but sun-
shine always dispelled his darkness, hope always
conquered his despair, and love always triumphed
over his sorrow and doubt. This is seen in
" The Two Voices," in such lines as these:

> " The highest mounted mind," he said,
> " Still sees the sacred morning spread
> The silent summit overhead.[108]

He could truthfully say of himself:

> I look at all things as they are
> But thro' a kind of glory.[109]

Even in the midst of his sorrow he classed himself with those who

> trust that somehow good,
> Will be the final goal of ill.[110]

He was hopeful that education would become
broad and enlightening where it was narrow and

---

[108] P. 31.
[109] " Will Waterproof," p. 112.
[110] " In Memoriam," LIV, p. 261.

benumbing.   His hope has since been justified by the facts.   He was troubled and bewildered by the mysteries of life, yet " he had a profound trust that when all is seen face to face, all will be seen as the best." [111]   He had an eternal hope for man, and that hope runs like a beam of light through the volumes of his verse.   He even spoke of " a hope for the world in the coming wars," [112] and in so doing was entirely consistent with his general teaching concerning the progress of the race.

He believed and taught that war is sometimes a necessity.   Then it is noble in any man

> To follow flying steps of Truth
> Across the brazen bridge of War.[113]

In defiance of the Quaker doctrine, he held it to be far from sin to strike down a public foe; yet in the same stanza he declares that " lawful and lawless war are scarcely even akin." [114]   " It is always better to fight for the good than to rail at the ill." [115]   He himself favored the Crimean War, and advocated an increase of the navy.

He felt very deeply, however, the horrors of war.   The French made of it a God; but he called

---

[111] *Memoir,* Vol. I, p. 316.
[112] " Maud," Part III, Sec. 6, St. 1.
[113] " Love Thou Thy Land," p. 65.
[114] " Maud," Part II, Secs. 5–10, p. 306.
[115] *Ibid.,* Part III, Sec. 6, St. v. p. 308.

it "wild war," "the child of Hell." [116] Force does not, cannot, determine questions of right and wrong. It is "the brute bullet" [117] that is the distinctive instrument employed by this "child of Hell," and the ruin it works is horrible beyond description. When war results in victory and you have killed your enemy, you must still remember that "your enemy was a man." [118] In short, the man

> Who loves war for war's own sake,
> Is fool, or crazed, or worse.[119]

War for the defense of native land and for liberty is sometimes necessary; but it is a sad necessity even then, in view of its fearful cost. Tennyson actually loathed it, and his dream of the future millennium included, as one of its conspicuous features, "universal ocean softly washing all her warless isles." [120] The highest service and the only justification of war are thus to make war forever impossible.

War, being destructive, is therefore only negatively and secondarily the servant of progress. A righteous war may overthrow tyrants and oppression, and by so doing clear the way for the

---

[116] "Third of February," p. 221.
[117] "Defense of Lucknow," p. 519.
[118] "Locksley Hall Sixty Years After," p. 563.
[119] "Epilogue," p. 570.
[120] "Locksley Hall Sixty Years After," p. 565.

onward march of true progress. It is peace with
honor that is the real friend of science, art, labor,
and all the nobler ministries of life. All the
special problems with which the sociologist deals
are significant because of their relation to the
progress of the individual and the race. It is to
be expected that Tennyson will deal with the
great principles underlying all these problems,
rather than attempt any unusual solutions of
them; that he will picture actual conditions
against the background of the noblest ideals.

Of the land in its relation to the welfare of
the people he has comparatively little to say.
The strong attachment of the landholders to
their ancestral estates is portrayed again and
again. The pathetic cry of Sir Richard, as he
thought of the possibility of losing the land upon
which generation after generation of his forbears
had lived, is one of many expressions of the love
of the Englishman for his inherited estate.[121]
The unfortunate condition of those whose farms
were encumbered by debt and too heavily taxed is
also frequently mentioned; but there is comparatively little to show that the poet had thought
seriously of the relation of the ownership of land
to the progress of a people. No one would ever
be led to study the fundamental nature of the land

[121] See "The Foresters," Act I, sc. 1, p. 841.

problem by reading the poems of Tennyson. In
" The Princess " one asks the question :

> Why should not the great Sirs,
> Give up their Parks some dozen times a year,
> To let the people breathe? [122]

In " The Promise of May," Dobson quotes a
" *hartist* " who cried out even among his oppo-
nents : " The land belongs to the people." [123]
Such fugitive words as these can have very little
social significance in such a study as we are making.

Tennyson's knowledge of science would naturally induce him to give great emphasis to the
power of environment in the development of the
life of the individual. He knew that this theory
of science was true in his own life, and believed
that it must be true in all lives. The poet said
with Ulysses : " I am a part of all that I have
met." [124] Yet when this teaching seemed to conflict with his conception of freedom, he positively
affirmed the superiority of the man to his sur-
roundings. In " In Memoriam " he speaks of
the man

> Who breaks his birth's invidious bar,
> And grasps the skirts of happy chance,

[122] " Conclusion," p. 217.
[123] Act I, p. 779.
[124] " Ulysses," p. 95.

And breasts the blows of circumstance,
And grapples with his evil star;

Who makes by force his merit known,
And lives to clutch the golden keys,
To mold a mighty state's decrees,
And shape the whisper of the throne.[125]

Thus, while recognizing the influence of environment in the development of a life, Tennyson put his emphasis upon the possible mastery of all untoward outward conditions by a soul that is free to aspire and to achieve.

The city was to Tennyson, as it is to almost all refined natures, both attractive and repulsive. He had words of praise to speak for the "busy town," though Hallam railed at it in scornful terms.[126] When his home was in High Beach, he liked the nearness of London, and often resorted thither to see his friends, Spedding, Fitzgerald, Kemble, and others.[127] The "central roar" of the great city had for him a peculiar charm. When he and his son went to the great world-metropolis, one of the first things they did was to walk to the Strand and Fleet Street.

On the other hand, there were features of city life which were positively repellent to him. These are frequently referred to by different char-

[125] LXIV, p. 263.
[126] "In Memoriam," LXXXIX, p. 271.
[127] *Memoir*, Vol. I, p. 150.

acters in the poems. Edwin Morris had but
" one oasis in the dust and drouth of city life." [128]
Another was delighted to turn from the city lying
" beneath the drift of smoke," to the oak standing in the open field.[129] The city clerk was
eager to get his little Margaret " from the giant
factoried city-gloom." [130] Tennyson urged Maurice to visit him at the Isle of Wight, for
that is " far from noise and smoke of town." [131]
When obliged to stay in the city, he often wished
himself " far away out of smoky London." [132]
These disagreeable physical features of city life
are only the material counterpart of social and
moral conditions even more repellent. The rich,
characterless man leaves his estate that " fulsome
Pleasure " may " drown his heart in the gross
mud-honey of town." [133] The " Ancient Sage "
had not lost his wisdom when he said: " Night
enough is there in yon dark city." [134] The one
who speaks in " Locksley Hall Sixty Years
After " paints the picture in colors that are dark,
but none too dark for the facts.[135]

[128] " Edwin Morris," p. 83.
[129] " The Talking Oak," p. 89.
[130] " Sea Dreams," p. 156.
[131] " To Rev. F. D. Maurice," p. 234.
[132] *Memoir*, Vol. I, p. 237.
[133] " Maud," XVI, 1.
[134] *Poems*, p. 551.
[135] P. 566.

To one who knows that such conditions as
those just described actually prevail it is no wonder that in the city the great problems of human
society seem to center.   When the " smouldering
fire of fever creeps across the rotted floor," it is
evident that the problem most imperatively demanding immediate solution is one of sanitation.
In " The Village Wife " one whose daughter had
died of fever said: " An I thowt 'twur the will
o' the Lord, but Miss Annie she said it wur
draäins." [136]   To drain the fen is as certainly a
social service as to raise the school.[137]   The ignorant in city and country are forever ascribing
disease to the will of the Lord, and forever neg-
lecting to whitewash their own cottages.[138]
Even the leprosy was probably not a legacy of the
crusades, as was commonly supposed, but was
caused by meager and unwholesome diet, miserable lodging and clothing, physical and moral
degradation.[139]   Such facts as these the poet did
not allow his readers to forget, nor the other
equally important fact that the health of the mind
is involved with the health of the body.[140]   He
believed that the housing of the poor was one of

[136] P. 514.
[137] " Locksley Hall Sixty Years After," p. 567.
[138] " The Promise of May," Act III, p. 795.
[139] Note, p. 825.
[140] *Memoir*, Vol. I, p. 241.

the great problems of human society.[141] The
need of an intelligent study of the problem is
indicated by such portrayals as that in " The
Promise of May," where Dan Smith complains
of the thin walls of the house in which as a servant he is obliged to live, the broken windows
which remain unmended even when the weather
is intensely cold, and the " missus " in a precari-
ous condition.[142] Such ignorance of sanitary
laws and of the hardships and sufferings of the
poorer classes Tennyson deplored and sought to
banish.

Of crime and criminals the poet made no special
or exhaustive study. Crime of various sorts is
referred to, though not described in any fulness,
in such poems as " Maud " and " Locksley Hall
Sixty Years After." " Rizpah " records the life
and hanging of one who robbed the mail.
Crimes against women are especially condemned
by the poet. King Arthur and the Knights of
the Round Table always stood ready to defend
helpless women who had been wronged by the
ignoble. Robin Hood is praised as one who
never wronged a maiden.[143] The rascal in " Sea
Dreams " is most vividly depicted partly because

[141] *Loc. cit.,* p. 249.
[142] Act III, p. 795.
[143] " The Foresters," Act III, sc. 1, p. 858.

the character is drawn from a man who grossly cheated Tennyson himself in early life.[144]

Different forms of punishment for violation of law are mentioned. Imprisonment was, of course, one of the most common. When Cranmer was put into prison, he found nothing to complain of in the prison fare.[145] On the other hand, Howard describes the horrible conditions under which certain prisoners were compelled to exist or to die, though these prisoners were heretics, rather than disturbers of the social order.

I have seen heretics of the poorer sort,
Expectant of the rack from day to day,
To whom the fire were welcome, lying chained,
In breathless dungeons over steaming sewers,
Fed with rank bread that crawl'd upon the tongue,
And putrid water, every drop a worm,
Until they died of rotted limbs; and then
Cast on the dung hill naked, and become
Hideously alive again from head to heel,
Made even the carrion-nosing mongrel vomit,
With hate and horror.[146]

Other terrible forms of torture are described in the fifth act of " Queen Mary." In the drama of " Harold," Guy says to Harold:

In our oubliettes
Thou shalt or rot or ransom.[147]

[144] *Memoir,* Vol. I, p. 429.
[145] " Queen Mary," Act IV, sc. 2, p. 627.
[146] Act IV, sc. 3, p. 634.
[147] Act II, sc. 1, p. 662.

In the biography mention is made of the fact that women who were found guilty of murdering their husbands, or of the other offenses comprised under the terms " high " or " petit treason," were publicly burned, by a law which was not abolished till 1790.[148]   Punishment by transportation is also mentioned.[149]

There is no evidence that Tennyson had ever studied carefully the relation of intemperance to crime, poverty, and social degradation.   He was not an advocate of total abstinence, and was not averse to wine and beer, and similar drinks, for himself.   It was not merely a poetic figure when he called upon all to drink to the health of the queen, to the " great cause of freedom " and " the great name of England! " [150]   There were times when he " yearned after a pint of pale ale." When he " drank scarcely any wine," it was a thing to be especially noted.[151]   He was disgusted enough when he saw the drunkenness at elections,[152] when he saw riflemen get drunk every night, and squabble and fight and disgrace themselves and their corps; [153] but the cause of all

[148] *Memoir*, Vol. I, p. 7.
[149] *Ibid.*, p. 290.
[150] " Hands All Round," p. 575.
[151] *Memoir*, Vol. I, p. 465.
[152] *Ibid.*, p. 350.
[153] *Ibid.*, pp. 463, 464.

this disorder and disgrace he apparently never discovered, nor did he discern its significance for social progress. One can but feel that this very obvious limitation upon his usually clear vision was largely due to his own personal habits. He said on one occasion that the first time he met Robertson, he could talk of nothing but beer, stating, by way of explanation, that this was " from pure nervousness." [154]

In the poems the whole subject receives scant mention, and this is one of the omissions that carry a message. To be sure, in " The Promise of May" the evils of workingmen wasting their wages at a pothouse are recognized, if not fully and powerfully pictured.[155] " The Northern Cobbler," [156] however, gives the most striking dramatic portrayal of the terrible results of the drink habit upon one who has become a slave to it. The old cobbler tells of his courtship and marriage, and of the happiness that followed until he was mastered by his passion for gin. Then he lost his customers, abused his wife and child, and injured his own household possessions. New light and life came to him only when he resolved with all his might to quit his evil way, and bring back peace and happiness to his home.

[154] *Ibid.*, p. 264.
[155] See especially Act III.
[156] P. 504.

He bought a bottle of gin and placed it before him in the shop. Then he faced it every day and became its master, as before it had mastered him. This is a picture not to be forgotten; but the importance to society at large of the individual problem which the old cobbler solved Tennyson did not reveal to the world nor appreciate himself. In this he is simply one of the crowd. He did not understand that the results of scientific investigation into the facts declare unmistakably that this is one of the great problems of the day, which cannot be left to the tender mercies of squint-brained cranks and decrepit old women. No poet has yet arisen to do for the enslaved millions of the liquor habit what Harriet Beecher Stowe did for the negro in her imaginative prose.

Tennyson was likewise born too soon to be greatly interested in the scientific administration of charity. He felt sincerely and deeply, so far as his knowledge went, the sorrows and sufferings of the poor, and pictured their condition and their needs with a sympathetic feeling that was genuine and strong. He praised those who gave of their substance to the sick and poverty-stricken. This praise was a part of the honor accorded Marie Alexandrovna, Duchess of Edinburgh, whose hand at home was gracious to her poor.[157] The divine ideals of service which were the glory

[157] "A Welcome," p. 225.

of the Round Table impelled Arthur to say to
Kay, the seneschal:

> Take thou my churl, and tend him curiously
> Like a King's heir, till all his hurts be whole.[158]

There was nothing nobler for the penitent, re-
deemed Guinevere to do than to give the remnant
of her life to the distribution of charity to the
poor and the sick.   Leonard, in " Locksley Hall
Sixty Years After," is exhorted to follow the example of him who " served the poor, and built
the cottage, raised the school and drained the
fen." [159]   Great admiration is given to Robin
Hood, who, though he robbed the rich, gave gen-
erously to the poor.   This virtue was also prominent in the life of Akbar, who was said to have
treated the poor for nothing.   Tennyson commended the church for preaching and practicing
this kind of charity, and giving to it all of the
sanction of the religious motive.   Cranmer was
really speaking for the church when he said:
" Give to the poor, ye give to God." [160]

The biographer declares that the poet reflected
much upon the great movements of philanthropy,
and his sympathy with them and with the gen-
erous impulse from which they sprang is evident
in his verse.   He felt that the English country

[158] " The Last Tournament," p. 445.
[159] P. 567.
[160] " Queen Mary," Act IV, sc. 3, p. 632.

gentlemen ought to be kinder to the poor, and said so plainly.[161]   He thought of the poor especially in cold weather, and feared that it would bring them great hardship.[162]   He thus helped to strengthen in English-speaking people the sense of obligation of the rich to the poor, and the impulse to charitable action.   He was the friend and supporter of great philanthropic movements and institutions, and in his own life practiced the principles he taught in his poems; but of the great problems of indoor and outdoor relief he wrote nothing, because of these he himself had no knowledge.

Tennyson believed in progress.   He believed this to be the assured destiny of the race and the world.   This is the fundamental tone in all his distinctive melodies.   The doctrine of evolution, which he championed so zealously in science, was really his doctrine of the movement of the world and of all life.   He was frank to say that, in his judgment, ruin attaches to everything material. To this degree he has rightly been called pessimistic.   Even wisdom as such cannot withstand evil, as the conflict of Merlin and Vivien illustrates.   The beast in man and in the race must be worked out, if real progress is ever to be attained.   It is only as the spiritual becomes dom-

[161] *Memoir*, Vol. I, p. 243.
[162] *Ibid.*, p. 261.

inant that the triumph of the higher is made certain and genuine progress becomes a fact in the
world.

What has already been said concerning Tennyson's appreciation of the great problems of the
soul and of life, of poverty and suffering and sin,
of all the forces that seem to make for decay and
ruin and death, is sufficient evidence that the poet
did not overlook or ignore the stern facts of existence in order to proclaim a hopeful doctrine of
progress.   The conditions that are portrayed in
" Maud " and the two " Locksley Halls " must
have been clearly seen and deeply felt by Tennyson before they could have been so vividly set
forth.   He saw realities, sad and disheartening
as they were.   He called upon all the Christmas
bells to ring out the false, the grief that saps the
mind, the feud of rich and poor, the ancient form
of party strife, the want, the care, the sin, the
faithless coldness of the times, the false pride in
place and blood, the civic slander and the spite,
the old shapes of foul disease, the narrowing lust
of gold, the thousand wars of old, the darkness
of the land.   He did this in order to ring in the
truth and love and peace of the Christ that is to
be.[163]   He knew that " the old order changeth,"
and oftentimes progress is retarded, and even
takes a backward and a downward step; but in

[163] " In Memoriam," CVI, p. 277.

the end " God fulfils himself " in the new order that comes to be established.

If these discouraging facts are frankly faced, and at the same time the poet maintains a stalwart faith in the ever-increasing triumph of the race and the final perfection of the world, he must have had a reason for the faith that was in him. What was that reason?

First, he believed that there are resident forces, as evolutionists say. in the world and in man which give assurance of progress. Though these forces are the abiding realities, they are not manifest to the one who does not look beneath the surface. They are perceived only by the one who has a passion for truth and who cannot be deceived by appearance. They are spiritual realities and are spiritually discerned. These remain when bodies and forms and creeds and institutions pass into ruin and decay. When " the old order changeth," as change it will, it is only that its spiritual essence may pass on and on into some higher form. It is thus that "God fulfils himself."

Again Tennyson had great faith in *time,* and what it can do for the individual and the world. He had little patience with revolutionists of any kind. Those who expect all things in an hour were not of his ilk. He was not discouraged when men said :

> The world is like a drunken man,
> Who cannot move straight to his end — but reels
> Now to the right, then as far to the left.[164]

In " The Ancient Sage " he asks:

> Who knows? or whether this earth-narrow life
> Be yet but yolk and forming in the shell?[165]

With time that " earth-narrow life " will broaden and reveal its essential nature and its highest mission.   The pessimist is such simply because he is blind.   He sees failure and wreck and loss, and does not see the triumph to which failure is but the prelude.   He does not see life in the large and the high achievement which only time can bring.   In 1842 Tennyson wrote:

> My faith is large in Time
> And that which shapes it to some perfect end.[166]

That faith grew stronger to the end of his life.

Moreover, he believed that what has actually been wrought up to the present time is more than prophecy; it is evidence of " the far things to be." He had read history and science to good purpose. He knew what the past had been.   Then he looked at his present, and saw what had actually been accomplished through the development of powers inherent in the world and life.

[164] " Queen Mary," Act IV, sc. 3, p. 634.
[165] P. 549.
[166] " Love and Duty," p. 93.

> All the years invent;
> Each month is various to present
> The world with some development.[167]

Looking backward, and then at the present, he saw clearly the direction of the movement.

> All things move. . . . .
> And human things returning on themselves
> Move onward leading up the golden year.[168]

When he wrote, " That which they have done but earnest of the things that they shall do," [169] he was only affirming that for which most positive evidence had been adduced. Men are constantly achieving. The brain grows with using. There is nothing lost to man.

> So that still garden of the souls
> In many a figured leaf enrolls
> The total world since life began.[170]

Then, since men are constantly attaining, and nothing is lost, progress is the inevitable conclusion.

Lastly, and most comprehensively, Tennyson believed in God. No one can write any part of the philosophy of the great poet and leave God out; for the presence and power of the Almighty in the world and society and the life of the indi-

[167] " The Two Voices," p. 31.
[168] " The Golden Year," p. 94.
[169] " Locksley Hall," p. 101.
[170] " In Memoriam," XLIII, p. 258.

vidual were an underlying principle in all his thinking. This fact revealed the order in seeming chaos, and the hidden purpose of experiences apparently meaningless and dark. When others were bewildered by failure and defeat he still walked in the light; for he held

> That men may rise on stepping stones
> Of their dead selves to higher things.

To those higher things God is forever calling his children, even out of the grave of their dead selves. Then no toil or suffering or sorrow stands by itself. It is a part of a larger whole, and gets its significance from its relation to the great consummation to which it contributes.

> I see in part
> That all, as in some piece of art,
> Is toil cooperant to an end.[171]

As it is with the individual, so it is with the great universe of which he is a part. " Thro ' the ages one increasing purpose runs." [172]   That purpose is ever being accomplished, because above and beyond all is

> That God which ever lives and loves,
> One God, one law, one element,
> And one far-off divine event,
> To which the whole creation moves.[173]

[171] *Ibid.,* CXXVIII, p. 283.
[172] " Locksley Hall," p. 101.
[173] " In Memoriam," p. 286.

CHAPTER IX

SUMMARY AND CONCLUSION

We have seen that literature and sociology are mutually helpful to each other in their great and inspiring tasks. Sociology gives to literature facts concerning the social life of individuals and of classes, and in return literature gives to sociology a concrete and dramatic presentation of the condition and needs of the time it attempts to portray. The misapprehensions which literature creates, sociology corrects by a careful record of the results of scientific investigation into social realities. Literature gives life and power to facts which of themselves are inert and dead, and brings these facts to the knowledge of multitudes who would otherwise be ignorant of them. These two great departments of human effort are, therefore, partners and not antagonists, each rendering to the other a service that is of great significance and value.

Literature is, however, only one of many documents to which the student of society must give careful attention. It is the helper, but never the ruler, of the worker in the social realm. Only as literature is true to the highest principles of its own art does it render a service for which the sociologist has any special reason to be grateful. When it attempts to "talk down," or becomes contented with slovenly homilies, it does nothing except degrade itself in the eyes of all beholders. It must study and reflect the past, giving vividness and reality to that which the chronicler coldly states. It must record the positive and the negative results of social experiments from which the principles of progress shall become more and more evident. It is a part of its mission to disclose tendencies which have not yet developed into recognized movements or alarming facts.

It is one of the special social functions of literature to call attention to existing wrongs and to disseminate intelligence concerning abuses. Thus it becomes an advance agent of reform; for no social wrong is ever righted until people are first made aware that a wrong exists, and made to *feel* the reality of the iniquity. It therefore does most effective work in the first stages of a reform, and often is forgotten by the time the labor it inspired has resulted in corrective legislation or a more righteous custom. The breeze which fans the spark into flame is unremembered when the attention of men is engrossed by the great conflagration. But when literature brings to self-consciousness the torpid, dormant society of its own day, it is rendering a social service of great magnitude. It cannot be ignored in any careful study of social forces.

Perhaps, however, the greatest aid which literature gives to the progress of society consists in its embodiment of the highest individual and social ideals. Makers of literature are not, as a rule, successful makers of social programs. They are rather revealers of an idealism which may seem visionary and impracticable, but which is in reality a call to the noblest achievements. This call people cannot and will not ignore. This is a mighty force making for advancement in human society. By the artistic, imaginative presentation of facts, conditions, needs, and ideals, the writer of literature becomes a social educator and reformer of great importance in the society whose life he touches.

It is therefore natural to expect that the writings of Alfred Tennyson will have social as well as literary significance. He lived at a time when the changes in industry and society were many and great. The discovery of the motive power of steam was a prelude to social transformations that made the nineteenth century conspicuous in the history of the world. Factories were established, foreign and colonial commerce greatly increased. Political reforms were carried out by

which the franchise was extended and political
tolerance gained for those of all religious faiths.
Trades unions were organized and great co-operative schemes successfully launched. The age
was marked by the growth of democracy, political liberty, and education. Our study reveals
to us in part how the poet influenced, and was
influenced by, this time of growth for the nation,
of suffering for the poor, of marvelous change
in social, industrial, and political life.

In any theory of society the conception of man
is fundamental. To Tennyson man is a being
whom God has made in his own image. He
has a distinct personality, however, which is
spiritual in its essential nature and is free in will.
He dwells in a body through which he is related
to the beasts and all the lower orders of creation.
He has therefore a twofold possibility. He has
angel instincts, which make him like to God, and
he has possibilities of sin and degradation which
are terrible to contemplate.

Man's duties and destinies are determined by
his nature and his highest capacities. He has
obligations to God, his Creator, and to man, his
brother. Being true to these obligations, he
moves toward the summit of his destiny, which
is too high to be fully attained in one brief age,
but demands an immortality. Man now is being
made. He carries in himself the results of the

evolution of the past and the prophecies of the developments of the future. Such men as Prince Albert are actual illustrations of the practicability of these high ideals, and give to us a faith in "the growing purpose of the sum of life," the noble destiny of the individual and the race. This is the man who lives and aspires and achieves, who is the unit of the family, of the government, and of every social institution.

Special importance attaches to the conception of woman in the social system. The society that cherishes a low ideal of the worth and mission of woman cannot itself attain a high mental and moral level. No woman created wholly by the imagination of Tennyson stands out from the company of her sisters as absolutely ideal. The noblest types of womanhood portrayed in the poems are taken from life and not from fancy. It is a significant thing that the poet found such women as Isabel in the world of the actual. He lays emphasis upon the fact that woman is not a lower species of man, but possesses her own nature and capacities, which should be developed in accordance with the laws of her own being. It is a mistake to speak of the man and the woman as either equals or unequals. They are diverse, and should have the education that will fit them to do in the best way the work to which they are called by their different tastes, capacities, and

talents.   Thus the poet lays great stress upon the
noble power of woman in her sex-relations.
The function of motherhood is exalted.   This is
a part of Tennyson's life-philosophy; for only in
love and service can the individual attain his own
highest development, and contribute his part to
the progress of the race.   This important and
highly honorable place which woman occupies in
the social body, makes the question of a higher
education, which shall fit her to accomplish her
mission in the noblest way, one of the great social
problems of the age.   To the careful study and
intelligent solution of this problem the poet called
the people of his time, with the strong conviction
of the reformer and the skilful appeal of the
artist.

In the family the man and the woman come
together in the primary social organization.
Here it is necessary that the freedom of each be
maintained, and at the same time that the good
of society be subserved.   To gain these ends, the
marriage bond is a necessity.   In every real spiritual union this bond is not a burden.   It is a
seal of the happiness of two souls who are coming to their highest development, and finding the
true riches of life, not in isolation, but in pure
and holy union.   If one suffers because of a hasty
or unwise marriage, that suffering should be endured, rather than imperil the great interests of

society by a disregard of the bond upon which the true social order depends.

One distinct danger that society has to recognize and meet is that which comes from marriage for money, or rank, or policy. Here the poet held the mirror up to his time, and disclosed the direful results of degrading so sacred an institution by such ignoble motives. The parties to such a marriage pay the penalty of this disobedience to the highest laws of spiritual union, and also degrade society of which they are a part. No one can read the poems of Tennyson which treat of this subject and be blind to the contempt he feels for the match which is barren of love and is prompted by selfish or unworthy aims. The marriage of true souls brings peace and happiness. If the persons are of unequal rank, the one of lower social position may find much in that fact to bring embarrassment and annoyance, but the love which is the heart of all true marriage is mightier than all distinctions of rank.

The principle of heredity is of very great importance in the family and in society. The child is not only influenced by the physical and psychical life of the parents, but also influences in turn the home and the school and the church — in fact, the whole social body. The training of the child for his work in the world is a social as well as a parental duty. To take mothers, to whom especially the care and nurture of children are intrusted, from their homes to labor in mines and factories for the support of the family is, therefore, a wrong to the child, to the family, and to society at large.

The ideal which one holds for society is largely determined by the ideal cherished for the individual. The universe is one, and to understand even the flower in the crannied wall is to know what God and man is. Each individual will is distinct and free, yet it has an eternal significance for every other. Good and evil are each, first individual, and then social. One's own country represents an extension of the family group, and for the advancement of the highest interests of this larger social organization the individual has a responsibility that is real and great.

To love one's country sincerely and intelligently is a necessary preparation for participation in the still larger brotherhood of mankind. This universal brotherhood is the true social ideal. The problem is to change the actual of the present into the ideal of the future.

That is a problem whose solution is difficult; for today there are many barriers separating man from his brother, and dividing society into different, and oftentimes antagonistic, classes. The distinctions of rank are external, and are by no means always a mark of gentleness and worth.

Rank and wealth help to divide class from class, and too often bring to their possessors the degradation which is born of luxury and excess, of false pride, and selfish disregard of the sorrows and sufferings of others. But, despite all that money can buy or titles can bring, joys and sorrows are common to rich and poor. Money and rank can do much less for a man than most people imagine. There are hardships which the poor alone suffer, and the principles of brotherhood lay upon the rich an obligation to give to their poorer brethren sympathy and aid. Poverty brings less actual suffering in the country than in the city, but wherever it is found, it gives to possessors of wealth the opportunity to sympathize and serve. This is the teaching of Tennyson's poems, and this was the practice of his life.

The poet never advocated the theories of communism. He did not believe in these himself, and when they are mentioned in his writings, it is only to reveal their foolish and impractical nature. He faced the gloomy facts of social and industrial life, but believed that these only imposed the obligation upon all members of society to live together as brethren. Penetrating all disguises and all deceptive appearances, he found the cause of social unrest and suffering and disorder in the selfish spirit that pervades society. When this ignoble spirit of selfishness is banished by the coming of the spirit of Christ, the spirit of love and service into human society, the vexing social problem will be solved and the millennial age will dawn.

While society is advancing from a lower to a higher stage of development, institutions are a necessity. These represent ideas and exist to meet a need. Their forms are largely dependent upon the conditions of the time in which they are, and change as ideas advance or needs pass away. Institutions decay, but the spirit that gave them life and power passes on into new and higher forms. Here, as everywhere, it is the external and formal which is transient, the inner and spiritual that is eternal.

The state is a social institution in which Tennyson had special interest. He believed the English government to be the best in the world, and had a peculiar horror of revolutions, and all sudden and violent change in the established social order. He recognized the necessity of having able officials and a pure court; for the spiritual and the political are indissolubly united. Moral depravity means ultimate political ruin. In an hereditary monarchy the king may be a tyrant, and in a republic the crowd may be equally despotic. Tennyson hated with equal fervor the tyranny of one and the tyranny of many. The queen was to him the ideal ruler, and in his

noblest verse he voiced the inarticulate loyalty
of the English people to their well-loved sovereign. The monarch should be loved by the people, and in return for this loyal devotion he should
give himself and his all to the kingdom he serves.

In the government the statesman stands next
to the ruler. It is his duty to understand the
needs of the people, and become a real leader in
the accomplishment of their worthiest ends. He
will despise lying and every form of dishonesty,
and seek above all things to know and live the
truth. If statesman and people swerve from the
path of honor, the poet, the man of vision, will
recall all to truth and duty. In this way the poet
and the statesman become partners in social service. Both these public servants should understand that in government, as everywhere else, all
law is primarily internal and spiritual. It is written in the very nature of things; yet, to be of
service to common men, it must have external
expression. When the law is broken with impunity by its subjects, no further evidence is
needed of the decay of the government. Laws
which only imperfectly express the principles of
social order should be changed from time to time,
as the ideas of people grow, and those inner and
eternal principles are more perfectly revealed.
All innovations should, however, come naturally
out of the experience of the past and lead the way

to higher achievements in the future. Every true statesman will be above the petty disputes and ignoble schemes of selfish factions. He will see the larger truths and be inspired by nobler aims.

The church is a social institution only second in importance to the state. God is the fundamental fact in the world and in life, and what men call religion is therefore a perfectly natural phenomenon. To make religion effective in practical life is the mission of the church. Those who follow " wandering fires " miss what is vital and essential in religion. The church should have truth as its standard, and love as its inspiring spirit. Tennyson sought for the truth which underlies all religions, and he believed that all these are in their highest elements vitally related to Christianity. Thus he contended for a creed that is broad as the truth, and which expresses itself in deeds of love and service rather than in narrow dogmas. His creed is written into his poems, but was never formulated in labeled articles of faith. He believed in God, in Christianity, and the established church, though he steadfastly refused to become a partisan of any creed or sect.

The corruptions and weaknesses of the church and its representatives he pictured with fearless candor. The priest who robs the poor, and lives in luxury and idleness and excess, stands in marked contrast with the faithful servant of the church who boldly proclaims the truth, ministers to the poor and sinful, and brings comfort and solace to the sick and dying. Maurice and Robertson were to him illustrations of what the clergyman should be and do in order to make the church a most efficient agent in social progress.

Progress, to be real, must mean the advancement, not of a favored class, but of the people as a whole. The question of the relation of democracy to progress is a very important and a very difficult one. In the poems the people are sometimes pictured as foolish, passionate, and false; but even then they are capable of training and development. In the past they have been oppressed and made to bear heavy burdens. It is not to be wondered at that they resented such treatment, and in time came to demand for themselves justice and a fair share of privilege and of power. This demand does not mean that every man is the equal of every other in natural endowments, and should be equal in material possessions. That is an absurdity. It does mean that every man should have a fair chance to be his best and to do what he is prepared to do.

Education thus becomes a most important factor in social progress; but this signifies much more than acquiring knowledge. True education will train one for the position in life he is destined to fill and will include the physical and spiritual as well as the intellectual. If it be true to its ideal, it will be pervaded by the spirit of love. It must give its blessings to the masses, that they may be prepared for the duties that are sure to come to them with the advance of the democratic idea. This gives special significance to the university-extension movement, and kindred schemes for the spread of popular education. The discoveries of science are vastly important in this new age. These teach us that the method of evolution is the true method of social progress. War for the defense of one's country or the righteous cause is sometimes a necessity, and the male children should therefore be trained to defend the nation in time of peril as well as to serve it in time of peace.

Tennyson faced the gloomy facts of life with genuine courage, and portrayed these in his poems; yet he was never a pessimist. He believed that the future has much light to shed upon dark realities of the present. Of the special social problems he spoke with the freedom always accorded the poet. He pictured the attachment of landowners to their ancestral estates, the gains and perils of city life, the consequences of disregard of sanitary laws, the power of environment in the development of the man, the causes and effects of crime, the forms of punishment used, and the necessity and beauty of a noble charity. Concerning some important themes he is silent. Seeing clearly, as he did, the foes of progress, he yet remained to the end of his life a consistent optimist; for he believed in the innate powers of the man made in the image of God, in the revelations and blessings that time can bring, in the splendid prophecy of present achievements, and in the unfailing wisdom and power and love of God.

In conclusion, then, we may safely affirm that Tennyson has rendered to the world a distinct social service, by portraying with clearness and beauty and power the time in which he lived. Anyone possessing the poems of the great laureate has at hand data from which he may learn the physical and psychical and political and social facts of the time which the verses have for their theme. The historical plays and poems record the life of a former age, and thus furnish material for the social study of a past epoch. "Locksley Hall" gives a fine dramatization of a certain period in the history of England. The fact that Tennyson treats despair so frequently and fully shows clearly a condition of the time which is full of meaning for the student of society. In general it may be said that, from the year 1835 until the year of his death, he based his poetry largely on the "broad and common interests of the time and of universal humanity," and such poems have permanent value in the social literature of the age.   The bitter experiences through which the cruelty of his critics caused him to pass gave him, after all, a deeper and fuller insight into the requirements of the time, and new power as a poet and prophet.[1]   Feeling as intensely as he did the " mechanic influence of the age, and its tendency to crush and overpower the spiritual in man;" [2] interested as he was in science, politics economic invention, philosophy, theology, philanthropy and reform, it is not surprising that these great themes entered into his writings, and made his verse a microcosm of the thought and action of his time.[3]

The value of what he has written is greatly enhanced by the fact that there is in it all an undertone of rational, intelligent optimism.   As one who knew him well said of him: " He does not cry out against the age as hopelessly bad, but tries to point out where it is bad, in order that each individual may do his best to redeem it; as the evils he denounces are individual, only to be cured by each man looking to his own heart. He denounced evil in all its shapes, especially

[1] *Memoir,* Vol. I, p. 123.
[2] *Ibid.,* p. 169.
[3] *Ibid.,* p. 185.

those considered venial by the world and society." [4]

In such poems as " Lady Clare," " The Lord of Burleigh," " Locksley Hall," " Maud," and " Locksley Hall Sixty Years After," Tennyson has given statements of some of the varied phases of the social problem. But these are only illustrations of the way in which this grave question enters into the writings of this great poetic genius. Even when he treats in a large way the war of sense with soul, as in " The Vision of Sin " and the " Idylls," he is portraying a conflict which is not an incidental but a vital part of the problem that is vexing society. The cause of the social difficulty he believed to be the selfish spirit which pervades the whole frame of society. This spirit manifests itself in a thousand forms, but the problem is fundamentally one. What he considered the two great social questions then pending in England (" the housing and education of the poor man before making him our master, and the higher education of women ") were to his mind simply the phases of the problem most imperatively demanding consideration at a given time. Linked with these questions are many, many others, any one of which may assume a relatively great importance with a change of social and industrial conditions.

[4] *Memoir,* Vol. I, p. 468.

The whole matter was one of very great serious-
ness to him — so serious that it pained him to
hear anyone speak lightly of it, even in jest.[5]

While it is true that Tennyson did not formulate a program warranted to cure all social ills,
he did point out very clearly a principle which
must be followed, if the problem is ever to be
solved.   The poems referred to in the preceding
paragraph contain their own suggestions of the
solutions of the problems they state.   Commerce
may do something to bring in the federation of
the world.   Even war for defense or liberty has
its mission at a certain stage in the evolution of
society.   When the Chartist and socialist agitations were alarming the country, he believed the
remedy was not in imprisonment, but in a widespread national education, in a more patriotic and
less partisan spirit in the press, in a partial adoption of free-trade principles, and in an increased
energy and sympathy among those who belonged
to the different forms of Christianity.[6]

But he understood that such measures are only
temporary expedients, which may ameliorate, but
which can never cure, the social disorders.   He
at first thought, with Shelley, that the cause of
social ills might be removed by lopping off those
institutions in which the selfish spirit manifests

[5] *Ibid.,* p. 205.
[6] *Ibid.,* p. 185.

itself. He soon learned, however, that that method would not bring about the desired result. He became convinced that we must implant another principle, with which selfishness cannot co-exist — a principle that, by its superior attractive power, will draw to itself the virtue and strength which selfishness had before absorbed. In this way the greed which produces crime and misery and every form of social disease will be banished through the expulsive power of the new and stronger and nobler spirit.[7] In the individual and in society it is love which is this redemptive principle. It manifests itself in disinterested service of country and of fellow-men. This is the redemptive principle in " Maud." This is " the Christ that is to be."

This may be called an attempt to solve the social problem by the power of an ideal. Be it so. It is an ideal that is thoroughly workable. It has a message for every individual, every family, every nation and all mankind. It is an ideal which is today actually uplifting our earth into the light. Telemachus is not the only one of whom it may be said: " His dream became a deed that woke the world.[8] In an age full of social wrong, it is true that

[7] *Memoir,* Vol. I, p. 69.
[8] " St. Telemachus," p. 878.

> wildest dreams
> Are but the needful preludes of the truth.[9]

The poet who can dream dreams of a diviner man and a purer and higher social state, and give to those dreams beauty and power in expression — such an one is rendering a service to society which is absolutely needful to the discovery and realization of the higher truth. Because men have dreamed in the past, we of today are working for the freedom of the individual through the development of his highest capacities, for the perfection of the family in the unity of love, for the purification of the nation through the unselfish efforts of citizen patriots, and for the parliament of man, the federation of the world. Because of those dreams, thousands of noble souls in many lands are proclaiming and living the doctrine: " All for each and each for all." [10]   The poet has so won men to believe in the reality of his ideals that today there are unnumbered multitudes who, in spite of wars and rumors of wars, are looking forward with confidence to the time when " all men's good " shall

> Be each man's rule, and universal Peace
> Lie like a shaft of light across the land,
> And like a lane of beams athwart the sea
> Thro' all the circle of the golden year.[11]

[9] " The Princess," p. 217.
[10] " Locksley Hall Sixty Years After," p. 564.
[11] " The Golden Year," p. 95.

Thus the poet who sees that the ideal is the real and who paints his visions and his dreams becomes a mighty force, making for social progress;

> For he sings of what the world will be
> When the years have died away.[12]

[12] "The Poet's Song," p. 124.

BIBLIOGRAPHY

The books and articles to which the author is especially indebted in the preparation of this volume are the following:

Arnold, Matthew. *Culture and Anarchy.*

Brooke, Stopford A. *Tennyson: His Art and Relation to Modern Life.*

Carlyle, Thomas. *Miscellaneous Essays.*

Cooke, Albert S. *Tennyson's The Princess.*

Escott, T. H. S. *Social Transformations of the Victorian Age.*

Francke, Kuno. *Social Forces in German Literature.*

Genung, John F. *Tennyson's In Memoriam.*

Gibbins, H. DeB. *The English People in the Nineteenth Century.*

Graham, P. A. *The Victorian Era.*

Harrison, Frederic. *Studies in Victorian Literature.*

Harrison, Frederic. *The Victorian Age.*

Luce, Morton. *A Handbook to the Works of Alfred Lord Tennyson.*

Mackenzie, Robert. *The Nineteenth Century: A History.*

Rawnsley, Rev. H. D. *Memories of the Tennysons.*

Ritchie, Anne Thackeray. *Records of Tennyson, Ruskin, Browning.*

Scudder, Vida D. *The Life of the Spirit in the Modern English Poets.*

Scudder, Vida D. *Social Ideals in English Letters.*

Sneath, E. Hershey. *The Mind of Tennyson.*

Stead, W. T. " Character Sketch of Tennyson." *Review of Reviews,* December, 1892.

Stedman, Edmund Clarence. *Victorian Poets.*

Swanwick, Anna. *Poets the Interpreters of Their Age.*

Tainsh, Edward Campbell. *A Study of the Works of Alfred Lord Tennyson.*

Tennyson, Hallam. *Alfred Lord Tennyson: A Memoir by His Son.* 2 vols. The Macmillan Co., 1897.

Tennyson, Alfred. *The Works of Alfred Lord Tennyson.* Macmillan & Co., 1894.

Van Dyke, Henry. *The Poetry of Tennyson.*

Walker, Hugh. *The Age of Tennyson.*

Walters, J. Cuming. *Tennyson; Poet, Philosopher, Idealist.*

Ward, William G. *Tennyson's Debt to Environment.*

Waugh, Arthur. *Alfred Lord Tennyson: A Study of His Life and Work.*

INDEX